Table of Contents

Unit 1 Vowel sound long /**a**/ 3
Unit 2 Vowel sound long /**e**/ 10
Unit 3 Vowel sound long /**i**/ 17
Unit 4 Vowel sound long /**o**/ 24
Unit 5 Vowel sound long /**u**/ 31
Unit 6 Review tests 243-254

Unit 7 **R**-controlled vowels / **är**/, /**ãr**/ 39
Unit 8 **R**-controlled vowels /**ėr**/ 46
Unit 9 Vowel sound /**ôr**/ 53
Unit 10 Vowel sound /**ô**/ 60
Unit 11 **R**-controlled vowel /**ər**/ 67
Unit 12 Review tests 255-266

Unit 13 Consonants /**c**/, /**g**/ 75
Unit 14 Consonants /**z**/, /**zh**/ 82
Unit 15 Consonants /**ch**/, /**sh**/ 89
Unit 16 Vowel /**ə**/ 96
Unit 17 Vowels / **ŭ**/, /**ū**/ 103
Unit 18 Review tests 267-278

Unit 19 Prefixes **dis, mis, un, ir, in, im** 111
Unit 20 Prefixes **non, en, mal, pre, pro, re** 118
Unit 21 Prefixes **ex, co, con, com, sub, mid** 125
Unit 22 Suffixes **er, or, ist, eer, ee, en, ant, ward** 132
Unit 23 Suffixes **ous, ment, able, ible, ance, ity, ence, ive** 139
Unit 24 Review tests 279-290

Unit 25 Sounds of **ch** 147
Unit 26 Sounds of **ch** 154
Unit 27 Antonyms 161
Unit 28 Homophones 168
Unit 29 Possessives 175
Unit 30 Review tests 291-302

Unit 31 Compound words 183
Unit 32 Consonant sounds /**sc**/ 190
Unit 33 **R**-controlled /**ear**/ 197
Unit 34 Plurals with /**f**/, /**ff**/, /**o**/ 204
Unit 35 Words with the same singular and plural 211
Unit 36 Review tests... 303-314

Spelling Glossary 219

My recommendation is to remove the answer key and unit tests before book is given to the student. Lesson plans are one page per day Monday through Wednesday. Thursday's work is writing the words three times each (sometimes two times each) on pages provided. The test is to be given on Friday. Give the review test for units indicated. It is recommended that one test per day be given for unit tests.

Grace and Glory Curriculum

Written by
Victoria Kays

Unit 1

These spelling words have the long **a vowel** sound.

1. crane
2. complain
3. grain
4. erase
5. behave
6. daily
7. sprain
8. celebrate
9. neighbor
10. freight
11. obey
12. eight
13. retake
14. nature
15. they
16. ache
17. faith
18. sleigh

The long **a** sound can be made in many ways. It can be made by the **a** + **consonant** + **e** pattern. It can be made by **a** + **consonant digraph** + **e** pattern. It can be made by the letters **ey**, **eigh**, and **ai**. The long **a** sound can also be made by the letter **a** at the end of an open syllable. An open syllable is one that ends with a vowel.

Unit 1

1. crane
2. complain
3. grain
4. erase
5. behave
6. daily
7. sprain
8. celebrate
9. neighbor
10. freight
11. obey
12. eight
13. retake
14. nature
15. they
16. ache
17. faith
18. sleigh

A. Write the spelling words in which the long **a** vowel sound is spelled by the **a + consonant + e** spelling pattern.

1. _____   2. _____

3. _____   4. _____

5. _____

B. Write the spelling words in which the long **a** vowel sound is spelled by the letters **ai**.

1. _____   2. _____

3. _____   4. _____

5. _____

C. Write the spelling words in which the long **a** vowel sound is spelled by the letters **ey**.

1. _____   2. _____

D. Write the spelling words in which the long **a** sound is spelled by **eigh**.

1. _____   2. _____

3. _____   4. _____

E. Write the spelling word that has the long **a** vowel sound spelled by the **a + consonant digraph + e** spelling pattern.

_____

F. Write the spelling word in which the **long a** vowel sound is spelled by the letter **a** in an open syllable.

_____

A. Find the misspelled word in each sentence. Write it correctly.

1. My neibor has his own tree cutting business. _____

2. Everyone should obay the rules. _____

3. There are several different kinds of birds in nachur. _____

4. We should read our Bibles daly. _____

5. A frate train wrecked. _____

B. Write the spelling word for each dictionary pronunciation.

1. (āt) _____ 2. (sprān) _____

3. (grān) _____ 4. (krān) _____

5. (slā) _____ 6. (thā) _____

7. (āk) _____ 8. (fāth) _____

C. Write these spelling words in syllables. Use your spelling glossary.

1. complain _____

2. erase _____

3. behave _____

4. celebrate _____

5. retake _____

D. Write these words in alphabetical order.
   freight   neighbor   sleigh   daily

1. _____ 3. _____

2. _____ 4. _____

Write the words that match each definition.

1. _____ to hurt a part of the body by twisting it.

2. _____ the outdoor world.

3. _____ cereal plants such as oats and wheat

4. _____ believing without proof

5. _____ a carriage mounted on runners for use on snow

6. _____ every day

7. _____ a train for carrying goods instead of people

8. _____ to have a party for a special reason

9. _____ a machine for lifting heavy objects

10. _____ to rub or wipe off

11. _____ to do as one is told; to follow orders

12. _____ to act correctly

13. _____ to talk about one's problems

14. _____ a person who lives nearby

15. _____ to take again

16. _____ a pain

17. _____ one more than seven

18. _____ the persons, things, or ideas spoken about

Write the spelling words three times.

1. crane _____ _____

   _____

2. complain _____ _____

   _____

3. grain _____ _____

   _____

4. erase _____ _____

   _____

5. behave _____ _____

   _____

6. daily _____ _____

   _____

7. sprain _____ _____

   _____

8. celebrate _____ _____

   _____

9. neighbor _____ _____

   _____

10. freight _____ _____

_____

11. obey _____ _____

_____

12. eight _____ _____

_____

13. retake _____ _____

_____

14. nature _____ _____

_____

15. they _____ _____

_____

16. ache _____ _____

_____

17. faith _____ _____

_____

18. sleigh _____ _____

_____

Unit 2

These spelling words have the long **e vowel** sound.

1. displease
2. disease
3. police
4. complete
5. steeple
6. beneath
7. legal
8. grease
9. peach
10. chief
11. concrete
12. believe
13. receive
14. feast
15. fever
16. indeed
17. ceiling
18. neither

The long **e** sound can be made in many ways. It can be made by the **e + consonant + e** pattern. It can be made by the letters **ee, ei, ie,** and **ea**. The long **e** sound can also be made by the leter **i** as in **police**. The long **e** sound can be made by the letter **e** at the end of an open syllable. An open syllable is one that ends with a vowel.

Unit 2

1. displease
2. disease
3. police
4. complete
5. steeple
6. beneath
7. legal
8. grease
9. peach
10. chief
11. concrete
12. believe
13. receive
14. feast
15. fever
16. indeed
17. ceiling
18. neither

A. Write the spelling words in which the long **e** vowel sound is spelled by the **e + consonant + e** spelling pattern.

1. _____ 2. _____

B. Write the spelling words in which the long **e** vowel sound is spelled by the letters **ea**.

1. _____ 2. _____

3. _____ 4. _____

5. _____ 6. _____

C. Write the spelling words in which the long **e** vowel sound is spelled by the letters **ee**.

1. _____ 2. _____

D. Write the spelling words in which the long **e** sound is spelled by the letters **ei**.

1. _____ 2. _____

3. _____

E. Write the spelling words in which the long **e** sound is spelled by the letters **ie**.

1. _____ 2. _____

F. Write the spelling words in which the long **e** sound is spelled in an open syllable.

1. _____ 2. _____

G. Write the spelling word whose long **e** sound is spelled with the letter **i**.

_____

A. Write the spelling word that is a synonym for each word.

1. trust _____ 2. cement _____

3. leader _____ 4. meal _____

5. sickness _____ 6. finish _____

B. Write the spelling word for each dictionary pronunciation.

1. (pēch) _____

2. (in dēd′) _____

3. (rĭ sēv′) _____

4. (grēs) _____

5. (dĭs plēs′) _____

6. (sēl′ ing) _____

C. Write these words in alphabetical order.

    police   steeple   beneath   legal   fever   neither

1. _____

2. _____

3. _____

4. _____

5. _____

6. _____

Write spelling words to complete the sentences.

1. Ed built a _____ for the church.

2. _____ cars have blue lights.

3. Use just a little bit of _____ when cooking eggs.

4. I painted the _____ of the kitchen.

5. The driveway was made of _____.

6. I was trying to _____ the lesson.

7. _____ of us enjoyed walking on the icy road.

8. Frankie was sick with a _____.

9. I did not intend to _____ the woman.

10. I hope Charles will _____ the letter.

11. Squanto was not an Indian _____.

12. Lawyers deal with _____ matters.

13. The first Thanksgiving _____ lasted three days.

14. Cancer is a terrible _____.

15. James crawled _____ the house to find the leak.

16. I _____ James is a hard worker.

17. A _____ is a fruit with little hairs on it.

18. Greg is _____ a busy man.

Write the spelling words three times.

1. displease _____ _____

   _____

2. disease _____ _____

   _____

3. police _____ _____

   _____

4. complete _____ _____

   _____

5. steeple _____ _____

   _____

6. beneath _____ _____

   _____

7. legal _____ _____

   _____

8. grease _____ _____

   _____

9. peach _____ _____

   _____

10. chief _____ _____

_____

11. concrete _____ _____

_____

12. believe _____ _____

_____

13. receive _____ _____

_____

14. feast _____ _____

_____

15. fever _____ _____

_____

16. indeed _____ _____

_____

17. ceiling _____ _____

_____

18. neither _____ _____

_____

Unit 3

These spelling words have the long **i vowel** sound.

1. bicycle
2. pirate
3. spy
4. nineteen
5. lightning
6. multiply
7. title
8. divide
9. polite
10. spider
11. silence
12. slight
13. triangle
14. reply
15. vitamin
16. type
17. style
18. ninety

The long **i** sound can be made in many ways. It can be made by the **i** + **consonant** + **e** pattern. It can be made by the letters **y** and **igh.** The long **i** sound can also be made by the letter **i** at the end of an open syllable. An open syllable is one that ends with a vowel.

Unit 3

1. bicycle
2. pirate
3. spy
4. nineteen
5. lightning
6. multiply
7. title
8. divide
9. polite
10. spider
11. silence
12. slight
13. triangle
14. reply
15. vitamin
16. type
17. style
18. ninety

A. Write the spelling words in which the long **i** vowel sound is spelled by the **i + consonant + e** spelling pattern.

1. _____ 2. _____

3. _____ 4. _____

B. Write the spelling words in which the long **i** vowel sound is spelled by the letters **igh**.

1. _____ 2. _____

C. Write the spelling words in which the long **i** vowel sound is spelled by the letter **y**.

1. _____ 2. _____

3. _____ 4. _____

5. _____

D. Write the spelling words in which the long **i** sound is spelled in an open syllable.

1. _____ 2. _____

3. _____ 4. _____

5. _____ 6. _____

7. _____

E. Vowels are missing from these words. Fill in the missing vowels.

1. p ___ r ___ t ___   2. n ___ n ___ t ___

3. v ___ t ___ m ___ n   4. b ___ c ___ cl ___

A. A word that has two or more syllables usually has one syllable that is stressed more than the others. The stressed syllable is said with greater force. The sign that shows this stress is called a **primary accent mark.** Write these words in syllables and put in the primary accent mark.

1. bicycle _____

2. lightning _____

3. divide _____

4. pirate _____

5. vitamin _____

6. triangle _____

B. Write the spelling word for each dictionary pronunciation.

1. (spī′ dər) _____

2. (nīn′ tēn) _____

3. (pə līt′) _____

4. (tī′ təl) _____

5. (nīn′ tē) _____

6. (mŭl′ tə plī) _____

7. (sī′ləns) _____

8. (stīl) _____

9. (slīt) _____

10. (rē plī′) _____

11. (tīp) _____ 12. (spī) _____

Write spelling words to complete the sentences.

1. A _____ can spin a web.

2. Ben Franklin proved that _____ is electricity.

3. Please _____ a letter for me on the computer.

4. Vickie rode a pink _____.

5. I hope you are able to _____ and _____ in math by the fifth grade.

6. If you subtract ten from one hundred, the answer would be _____.

7. A _____ has three sides.

8. The absence of noise is _____.

9. We should be _____ to visitors.

10. What _____ do you want your hair fixed?

11. Were you sent to _____ on someone here?

12. What was his _____ to your question?

13. You could pretend you are a _____ on a ship.

14. What is the _____ of the story?

15. James was _____ when we started dating.

16. There was more than a _____ difference in those twins.

17. Please take your _____ C every day.

21

Write the spelling words three times.

1. bicycle _____ _____

   _____

2. pirate _____ _____

   _____

3. spy _____ _____

   _____

4. nineteen _____ _____

   _____

5. lightning _____ _____

   _____

6. multiply _____ _____

   _____

7. title _____ _____

   _____

8. divide _____ _____

   _____

9. polite _____ _____

   _____

10. spider _____ _____

_____

11. silence _____ _____

_____

12. slight _____ _____

_____

13. triangle _____ _____

_____

14. reply _____ _____

_____

15. vitamin _____ _____

_____

16. type _____ _____

_____

17. style _____ _____

_____

18. ninety _____ _____

_____

Unit 4

These spelling words have the long **o vowel** sound.

1. thrown
2. grocery
3. golden
4. roam
5. total
6. growth
7. jumbo
8. roast
9. hollow
10. focus
11. quotation
12. postpone
13. arrow
14. locate
15. grove
16. studio
17. shallow
18. lotion

The long **o** sound can be made in many ways. It can be made by the **o** + **consonant** + **e** pattern. It can be made by the letters **ow** and **oa**. The long **o** sound can also be made by the letter **o** at the end of an open syllable. It can also be made by an **o** in the middle of a word.

Unit 4

1. thrown
2. grocery
3. golden
4. roam
5. total
6. growth
7. jumbo
8. roast
9. hollow
10. focus
11. quotation
12. postpone
13. arrow
14. locate
15. grove
16. studio
17. shallow
18. lotion

A. Write the spelling words in which the long **o** vowel sound is spelled by the **o + consonant + e** spelling pattern.

1. _____   2. _____

B. Write the spelling words in which the long **o** vowel sound is spelled by the letters **oa**.

1. _____   2. _____

C. Write the spelling words in which the long **o** vowel sound is spelled by the letters **ow**.

1. _____   2. _____

3. _____   4. _____

5. _____

D. Write the spelling words in which the long **o** sound is spelled in an open syllable.

1. _____   2. _____

3. _____   4. _____

5. _____   6. _____

7. _____   8. _____

E. Write the spelling words in which the long **o** sound is in the middle of the word and spelled by the letter **o**.

1. _____   2. _____

F. Write the spelling word that has two long **o**'s in it.

_____

A. A **base word** is a word to which prefixes or suffixes can be added. Write the base word for each of these words.

1. relocate _____
2. groceries _____
3. arrows _____
4. groves _____
5. shallowness _____
6. roasting _____
7. hollowed _____
8. jumbos _____

B. One word in each set is misspelled. Write the misspelled word correctly.

1. thrown, focus, quotetion _____
2. goldan, total, lotion _____
3. roem, studio, growth _____
4. postpone, totle, thrown _____
5. grocery, roast, fokus _____
6. studeo, locate, golden _____
7. hollow, groath, shallow _____
8. lotoin, jumbo, arrow _____
9. grove, postpoan, locate _____
10. grocery, jumbo, throan _____

27

Write the spelling word that fits each definition.

1. _____ a person's exact words

2. _____ large

3. _____ to find something

4. _____ having a bright yellow color

5. _____ to have cast off something

6. _____ to put off doing something; delay

7. _____ not deep

8. _____ the central point of attention

9. _____ the sum of all parts; to add up

10. _____ nothing but air on the inside

11. _____ a small group of trees

12. _____ a store that sells food

13. _____ to go from place to place without plans

14. _____ the activity of growing

15. _____ to cook meat in an oven

16. _____ a pointed stick that is shot from a bow

17. _____ a place from where radio shows are broadcasts

18. _____ a liquid applied to dry skin

Write the spelling words three times.

1. thrown _____ _____

   _____

2. grocery _____ _____

   _____

3. golden _____ _____

   _____

4. roam _____ _____

   _____

5. total _____ _____

   _____

6. growth _____ _____

   _____

7. jumbo _____ _____

   _____

8. roast _____ _____

   _____

9. hollow _____ _____

   _____

10. focus _____ _____

_____

11. quotation _____ _____

_____

12. postpone _____ _____

_____

13. arrow _____ _____

_____

14. locate _____ _____

_____

15. grove _____ _____

_____

16. studio _____ _____

_____

17. shallow _____ _____

_____

18. lotion _____ _____

_____

Unit 5

These spelling words have the long **u vowel** sound.

1. stew
2. loose
3. truth
4. blew
5. canoe
6. duty
7. fruit
8. poodle
9. crew
10. salute
11. clue
12. group
13. introduce
14. tune
15. suitcase
16. tooth
17. foolish
18. June

The long **u** sound can be made in many ways. It can be made by the **u** + **consonant** + **e** pattern. It can also be made by the letters **ew**, **oo**, **oe**, **ue**, and **ou**. It can also be made by the letter **u** in the middle of a word.

Unit 5

1. stew
2. loose
3. truth
4. blew
5. canoe
6. duty
7. fruit
8. poodle
9. crew
10. salute
11. clue
12. group
13. introduce
14. tune
15. suitcase
16. tooth
17. foolish
18. June

A. Write the spelling words in which the long **u** vowel sound is spelled by the **u + consonant + e** spelling pattern.

1. _____ 2. _____

3. _____ 4. _____

B. Write the spelling words in which the long **u** vowel sound is spelled by the letters **ew**.

1. _____ 2. _____

3. _____

C. Write the spelling words in which the long **u** vowel sound is spelled by the letters **oo**.

1. _____ 2. _____

3. _____ 4. _____

D. Write the words in which the long **u** sound is spelled by the letter **u** in the middle of the word.

1. _____ 2. _____

E. Write the spelling word that has the long **u** sound spelled **oe**.

_____

F. Write the spelling word that has the long **u** sound spelled **ou**.

_____

G. Write the words in which the **long u** sound is spelled by two vowels of which the first one is **u**.

1. _____ 2. _____

3. _____

A. Write the spelling word for each dictionary pronunciation.

1. (trüth) _____ 2. (tün) _____

3. (pü′ dəl) _____

4. (kə nü′) _____

5. (früt) _____ 6. (klü) _____

7. (jün) _____ 8. (stü) _____

B. Write these words in syllables. Include the accent marks. Use your glossary.

1. duty _____ 2. salute _____

3. introduce _____

4. suitcase _____

5. foolish _____

C. Find these words in your spelling glossary. Write their part of speech.

1. loose _____ 2. blew _____

3. crew _____ 4. group _____

5. tooth _____ 6. foolish _____

D. Write these words in alphabetical order.

    stew   canoe   group   clue

1. _____ 3. _____

2. _____ 4. _____

A. Fill in the blanks with spelling words in which both have the same spelling of the **long u** sound.

1. Wendy had a _____ _____ in her mouth.

2. It is your _____ to always tell the _____.

3. Because it was hot, Donna probably _____ the _____ to cool it.

4. The _____ _____ barked at me.

5. Did you pack some _____ in your _____ to eat?

6. Can you sing a _____ in the month of _____?

B. Complete the sentences with spelling words.

1. The kayak looked like a small _____.

2. Was Chris a _____ member on the boat?

3. Teri wanted to _____ her son to me.

4. Can you give me a _____ of what you're doing?

5. Many soldiers will _____ an army officer.

6. We sat together as a _____.

Write the spelling words three times.

1. stew _____ _____

    _____

2. loose _____ _____

    _____

3. truth _____ _____

    _____

4. blew _____ _____

    _____

5. canoe _____ _____

    _____

6. duty _____ _____

    _____

7. fruit _____ _____

    _____

8. poodle _____ _____

    _____

9. crew _____ _____

    _____

10. salute _____ _____

_____

11. clue _____ _____

_____

12. group _____ _____

_____

13. introduce _____ _____

_____

14. tune _____ _____

_____

15. suitcase _____ _____

_____

16. tooth _____ _____

_____

17. foolish _____ _____

_____

18. June _____ _____

_____

Unit 6
Review

Ask your teacher for each test and record your grade after you have taken the test.

Part 1 Grade _____

Part 2 Grade _____

Part 3 Grade _____

Part 4 Grade _____

Unit 7

These spelling words have **r- controlled vowel** sounds.

1. apartment
2. cargo
3. alarm
4. harness
5. target
6. careless
7. farther
8. harbor
9. pardon
10. spare
11. argue
12. airline
13. flare
14. repair
15. compare
16. spark
17. millionaire
18. aquarium

When a vowel is followed by the letter **r**, the vowel sound is changed slightly. The words in this unit have the **r-controlled** vowel sounds like those in **care** and **car**. The **r-controlled** vowel sound you hear in **car** is often spelled by the letters **ar** as in **mark.** The r-controlled vowel sound you hear in **care** can be spelled by the letters **are**, **air**, **aire**, and sometimes **ar** as in **aquarium**.

Unit 7

1. apartment
2. cargo
3. alarm
4. harness
5. target
6. careless
7. farther
8. harbor
9. pardon
10. spare
11. argue
12. airline
13. flare
14. repair
15. compare
16. spark
17. millionaire
18. aquarium

A. Write the spelling words in which the letters **air** or **aire** spell the **r**-controlled vowel sound you hear in **care**.

1. _____ 2. _____

3. _____

B. Write the spelling words in which the letters **ar** spell the **r**-controlled vowel sound you hear in **car**.

1. _____ 2. _____

3. _____ 4. _____

5. _____ 6. _____

7. _____ 8. _____

9. _____ 10. _____

C. Write the spelling words in which the letters **are** spell the **r**-controlled vowel sound you hear in **care**.

1. _____ 2. _____

3. _____ 4. _____

D. Write the spelling word in which the letters **ar** spell the **r**-controlled vowel sound you hear in **care**.

_____

E. Write the spelling words that have double letters.

1. _____ 2. _____

3. _____

A. Write the spelling word for each dictionary pronunciation.

1. (flâr) _____ 2. (ə lärm′) _____

3. (ə kwâr′ ĭ ŭm) _____

4. (spärk) _____ 5. (tär′ gĭt) _____

6. (här′ nĭs) _____

B. Write the spelling word that is an antonym for each word.

1. break _____ 2. careful _____

3. closer _____

C. Write the word that is a synonym for each word.

1. port _____

2. forgive _____

3. freight _____

4. save _____

5. quarrel _____

D. Write these words in syllables. Use your spelling glossary.

1. apartment _____

2. airline _____

3. compare _____

4. millionaire _____

Write the words that match each definition.

1. _____ a greater distance

2. _____ to fix something

3. _____ a goal for shooting

4. _____ one or more rooms used to live in

5. _____ an airplane company

6. _____ a very rich person

7. _____ a signal that gives a warning

8. _____ extra; to save

9. _____ goods carried by ship

10. _____ to discuss with someone who disagrees

11. _____ to determine how things are different

12. _____ an area where ships can dock

13. _____ a glass container where fish are kept

14. _____ a piece of leather used to hitch a horse

15. _____ not being careful

16. _____ to excuse; to forgive

17. _____ to flame suddenly

18. _____ a small bit of fire

Write the spelling words three times.

1. apartment _____ _____

 _____

2. cargo _____ _____

 _____

3. alarm _____ _____

 _____

4. harness _____ _____

 _____

5. target _____ _____

 _____

6. careless _____ _____

 _____

7. farther _____ _____

 _____

8. harbor _____ _____

 _____

9. pardon _____ _____

 _____

10. spare _____ _____

       _____

11. argue _____ _____

       _____

12. airline _____ _____

       _____

13. flare _____ _____

       _____

14. repair _____ _____

       _____

15. compare _____ _____

       _____

16. spark _____ _____

       _____

17. millionaire_____ _____

       _____

18. aquarium _____ _____

       _____

Unit 8

These spelling words have **r- controlled vowel** sounds.

1. surfboard
2. curly
3. service
4. curve
5. purse
6. search
7. birth
8. injure
9. nerve
10. research
11. flirt
12. clerk
13. thirteen
14. journey
15. verse
16. alert
17. purple
18. detergent

When a vowel is followed by the letter **r**, the vowel sound is changed slightly. The words in this unit have the **r**-controlled vowel sound like that in the word **term**. This **r**-controlled vowel sound can be spelled by the letters **er, ur, ear, ir**, and **our**.

Unit 8

1. surfboard
2. curly
3. service
4. curve
5. purse
6. search
7. birth
8. injure
9. nerve
10. research
11. flirt
12. clerk
13. thirteen
14. journey
15. verse
16. alert
17. purple
18. detergent

A. Write the spelling words in which the letters **er** spell the **r**-controlled vowel sound you hear in **term**.

1. _____ 2. _____

3. _____ 4. _____

5. _____ 6. _____

B. Write the spelling words in which the letters **ur** spell the **r**-controlled vowel sound you hear in **term**.

1. _____ 2. _____

3. _____ 4. _____

5. _____ 6. _____

C. Write the spelling words in which the letters **ir** spell the **r**-controlled vowel sound you hear in **term**.

1. _____ 2. _____

3. _____

D. Write the spelling words in which the letters **ear** spell the **r**-controlled vowel sound you hear in **term**.

1. _____ 2. _____

E. Write the spelling word in which the letters **our** spell the **r**-controlled vowel sound you hear in **term**.

_____

A. Write the spelling word for each dictionary pronunciation.

1. (flėrt) _____ 2. (nėrv) _____

3. (bėrth) _____ 4. (vėrs) _____

5. (kėrv) _____ 6. (pėrs) _____

7. (sėrch) _____ 8. (klėrk) _____

B. Write these spelling words in syllables. Use your spelling glossary.

1. surfboard _____

2. service _____

3. injure _____

4. research _____

5. thirteen _____

6. journey _____

7. alert _____

8. purple _____

9. detergent _____

C. Underline the spelling word in each sentence. Write its part of speech.

1. The clerk took our money. _____

2. I have a purple dress. _____

3. Jimmy had curly hair. _____

4. Do you have thirteen dollars? _____

Complete the sentences with spelling words.

1. Columbus made a _____ to find the Indies.

2. The preacher began to read at _____ eleven.

3. A child becomes a teenager at _____ years old.

4. The book of Luke tells about the _____ of Jesus.

5. We owned both houses on each side of the _____.

6. Is Kim's hair naturally _____?

7. What kind of _____ do you use to wash clothes?

8. I had pictures and money in my _____.

9. Be careful to not _____ yourself.

10. You need to stay _____ while driving.

11. Sometimes a boy will _____ with a girl if he likes her.

12. A pinched _____ in your back can cause pain.

13. We were in a church _____ Friday morning.

14. Would you like to be a _____ in the county government?

15. A bruise can be the color of _____.

16. I have never ridden a _____ in the ocean.

17. I do not like to have to _____ for my keys.

18. Did you _____ the life of Abraham Lincoln?

Write the spelling words three times.

1. surfboard _____ _____
   _____

2. curly _____ _____
   _____

3. service _____ _____
   _____

4. curve _____ _____
   _____

5. purse _____ _____
   _____

6. search _____ _____
   _____

7. birth _____ _____
   _____

8. injure _____ _____
   _____

9. nerve _____ _____
   _____

10. research _____   _____

_____

11. flirt _____   _____

_____

12. clerk _____   _____

_____

13. thirteen _____   _____

_____

14. journey _____   _____

_____

15. verse _____   _____

_____

16. alert _____   _____

_____

17. purple _____   _____

_____

18. detergent _____   _____

_____

Unit 9

These spelling words have **r- controlled vowel** sounds.

1. sword
2. shorten
3. explore
4. seashore
5. forty
6. chores
7. orbit
8. northern
9. bore
10. portable
11. normal
12. force
13. forbid
14. pork
15. orchard
16. ordinary
17. support
18. border

When a vowel is followed by the letter **r**, the vowel sound is changed slightly. The words in this unit have the **r-controlled vowel** sound like that in the word **door**. This **r-controlled vowel** sound can be spelled by the letters **or**, and **ore**.

Unit 9

1. sword
2. shorten
3. explore
4. seashore
5. forty
6. chores
7. orbit
8. northern
9. bore
10. portable
11. normal
12. force
13. forbid
14. pork
15. orchard
16. ordinary
17. support
18. border

A. Write the one-syllable spelling words that have the **or** sound.

1. _____ 2. _____

3. _____ 4. _____

5. _____

B. Write the two-syllable spelling words that have the **or** sound.

1. _____ 2. _____

3. _____ 4. _____

5. _____ 6. _____

7. _____ 8. _____

9. _____ 10. _____

11. _____

C. Write the three-syllable spelling word.

_____

D. Write the four-syllable spelling word.

_____

E. Letters are missing from these spelling words. Fill in the missing letters.

1. s ___ ___ ___ ___   2. ___ ___ ___ ___ ___ en

3. ___ ___ ___ ___ y   4. ___ ___ bit

5. ___ ___ ___ bid   6. ___ ___ ___ ___ ___ ern

55

A. Write the word for each dictionary pronunciation.

1. (ôr′ bĭt) _____

2. (pôrk) _____ 3. (chôrs) _____

4. (ôrd′ ən ĕr′ ē) _____

5. (sôrd) _____ 6. (bôr) _____

7. (ôr′ chėrd) _____

8. (shôrt′ ən) _____

B. One word in each set is misspelled. Write the word correctly.

1. explore, fourty, border _____

2. seeshore, support, force _____

3. northern, bordur, forbid _____

4. normal, shorten, portabel _____

5. explor, forbid, sword _____

6. chores, northen, orbit _____

7. shorten, suport, orchard _____

8. seashore, chores, forse _____

C. Write the word that fits each definition.

1. _____ of the usual standard; ordinary; regular

2. _____ not to allow

A. Complete the story with spelling words.

Many children may have (1) _____ to do at home in winter. They do not have much time to (2) _____ the earth. It is not (3) _____ to have snow on March 1 unless you live in the north on the (4) _____ of the Atlantic Ocean. You might even have (5) _____ inches of snow. It is not (6) _____ to have ten feet of snow in March. Your mother might (7) _____ you to go outside if you have too much snow. If you were to go outside, you might have to (8) _____ the door open. However, watching movies all day might (9) _____ you, so you might want to go ice skating. If you do, do not take a (10) _____ with you to cut the ice. You might want to (11) _____ your stay if you get too cold. Take a stick with you for (12) _____ in case you fall.

B. Complete the sentences with spelling words.

1. You may take a _____ radio with you if you want to sit by the _____.

2. Do not eat _____ meat in an apple _____.

3. You may _____ the earth in the _____ Hemisphere.

57

Write the spelling words three times.

1. sword _____ _____

   _____

2. shorten _____ _____

   _____

3. explore _____ _____

   _____

4. seashore _____ _____

   _____

5. forty _____ _____

   _____

6. chores _____ _____

   _____

7. orbit _____ _____

   _____

8. northern _____ _____

   _____

9. bore _____ _____

   _____

10. portable _____ _____

_____

11. normal _____ _____

_____

12. force _____ _____

_____

13. forbid _____ _____

_____

14. pork _____ _____

_____

15. orchard _____ _____

_____

16. ordinary _____ _____

_____

17. support _____ _____

_____

18. border _____ _____

_____

Unit 10

1. cause
2. because
3. haul
4. awful
5. automatic
6. sawdust
7. brought
8. paws
9. cough
10. fought
11. sawmill
12. laundry
13. author
14. ought
15. autumn
16. automobile
17. sought
18. bought

These spelling words have the vowel sound you hear in **all**.
This sound can be spelled by the letters **au**, **aw,** or **ou**.

Unit 10

1. cause
2. because
3. haul
4. awful
5. automatic
6. sawdust
7. brought
8. paws
9. cough
10. fought
11. sawmill
12. laundry
13. author
14. ought
15. autumn
16. automobile
17. sought
18. bought

A. Write the spelling words in which the letters **au** spell the vowel sound you hear in **all**.

1. _____ 2. _____

3. _____ 4. _____

5. _____ 6. _____

7. _____ 8. _____

B. Write the spelling words in which the letters **aw** spell the vowel sound you hear in **all**.

1. _____ 2. _____

3. _____ 4. _____

C. Write the spelling words in which the letters **ou** spell the vowel sound you hear in **all**.

1. _____ 2. _____

3. _____ 4. _____

5. _____ 6. _____

D. Write the spelling words that begin with the vowel sound you hear in **all**.

1. _____ 2. _____

3. _____ 4. _____

5. _____ 6. _____

A. Write these words in alphabetical order.

awful   automatic   author   autumn   automobile

bought   because   brought   cause   cough

1. _____

2. _____

3. _____

4. _____

5. _____

6. _____

7. _____

8. _____

9. _____

10. _____

B. Find these words in your spelling glossary. Write its part of speech.

1. haul _____ 2. sawdust _____

3. paws _____ 4. fought _____

5. sawmill _____ 6. laundry _____

7. ought _____ 8. sought _____

Write the word that fits each definition.

1. _____ past tense of seek

2. _____ a vehicle that can be driven

3. _____ an animal's feet

4. _____ what makes something happen

5. _____ past tense of bring

6. _____ to drag or carry heavy objects

7. _____ a building where logs are cut

8. _____ the fall season between summer and winter

9. _____ able to work by itself

10. _____ a place where clothes are washed

11. _____ for the reason that

12. _____ a person who writes stories

13. _____ terrible

14. _____ a sudden forcing of air through the throat

15. _____ did buy

16. _____ flecks of ground-up wood

17. _____ did fight

18. _____ should

Write the spelling words three times.

1. cause _____ _____

   _____

2. because _____ _____

   _____

3. haul _____ _____

   _____

4. awful _____ _____

   _____

5. automatic _____ _____

   _____

6. sawdust _____ _____

   _____

7. brought _____ _____

   _____

8. paws _____ _____

   _____

9. cough _____ _____

   _____

10. fought _____ _____

_____

11. sawmill _____ _____

_____

12. laundry _____ _____

_____

13. author _____ _____

_____

14. ought _____ _____

_____

15. autumn _____ _____

_____

16. automobile _____

_____

17. sought _____ _____

_____

18. bought _____ _____

_____

Unit 11

1. major
2. corner
3. capital
4. slipper
5. crumble
6. popular
7. grammar
8. shelter
9. stable
10. label
11. festival
12. alligator
13. similar
14. chisel
15. bridle
16. nickel
17. flannel
18. hospital

All of these spelling words contain a **schwa** sound. The **schwa** sound is an unstressed vowel sound. The schwa sound occurs only in syllables that have no accent. In the pronunciation key of most dictionaries, the schwa sound is spelled with the symbol ə. The schwa sound can be made by the vowels **a**, **e**, or **o**.

Unit 11

1. major
2. corner
3. capital
4. slipper
5. crumble
6. popular
7. grammar
8. shelter
9. stable
10. label
11. festival
12. alligator
13. similar
14. chisel
15. bridle
16. nickel
17. flannel
18. hospital

A. Write the spelling words in which the letters **le** spell the **schwa + l** sound.

1. _____ 2. _____

3. _____

B. Write the spelling words in which the letters **el** spell the **schwa + l** sound.

1. _____ 2. _____

3. _____ 4. _____

C. Write the spelling words in which the letters **al** spell the **schwa + l** sound.

1. _____ 2. _____

3. _____

D. Write the spelling words in which the letters **or** spell the **schwa + r** sound.

1. _____ 2. _____

E. Write the spelling words in which the letters **ar** spell the **schwa + r** sound.

1. _____ 2. _____

3. _____

F. Write the spelling words in which the letters **er** spell the **schwa + r** sound.

1. _____ 2. _____

3. _____

G. Write the spelling words with double letters.

1. _____ 2. _____

3. _____ 4. _____

A. Write these spelling words in syllables. Put in the accent marks. Use your spelling glossary.

1. label _____ 2. major _____

3. stable _____ 4. similar _____

5. crumble _____

B. Write the spelling word for each dictionary pronunciation.

1. (fĕs′ tə vəl) _____

2. (hŏs′ pĭ təl) _____

3. (brī′ dəl) _____

4. (shĕl′ tər) _____

5. (kôr′ nər) _____

6. (slĭp′ ər) _____

7. (grăm′ ər) _____

8. (ăl′ ə gā tər) _____

C. One word in each set is misspelled. Write the word correctly.

1. slipper, capetal, grammar _____

2. chizel, similar, hospital _____

3. flanel, label, festival _____

4. bridle, major, popelar _____

5. stable, nickle, alligator _____

A. Complete the story with spelling words.

Jesus was not born in a (1) _____.

He was born in a (2) _____. A stable is a small

(3) _____ for animals. He was wrapped in swaddling

clothes which was probably (4) _____ to

(5) _____. Even though this was a

(6) _____ event, there was no (7) _____

held for him. His parents might not have spoken proper

(8) _____, but Jesus is still the most

(9) _____ baby that was ever born.

B. Complete the sentences with spelling words. You will need to add **s** to one word.

1. James used a wood _____ to trim a place for a hinge.

2. I wore blue _____ on my feet.

3. The _____ of the United States is Washington D. C.

4. An _____ is similar to a crocodile.

5. A _____ is worth five cents.

6. Do not _____ bread on the floor.

7. Use a _____ when riding a horse.

8. Put a name _____ on each dish you take to the dinner.

9. There is a stop sign at the _____.

Write the spelling words three times.

1. major _____ _____

   _____

2. corner _____ _____

   _____

3. capital _____ _____

   _____

4. slipper _____ _____

   _____

5. crumble _____ _____

   _____

6. popular _____ _____

   _____

7. grammar _____ _____

   _____

8. shelter _____ _____

   _____

9. stable _____ _____

   _____

10. label _____ _____

_____

11. festival _____ _____

_____

12. alligator _____ _____

_____

13. similar _____ _____

_____

14. chisel _____ _____

_____

15. bridle _____ _____

_____

16. nickel _____ _____

_____

17. flannel _____ _____

_____

18. hospital _____ _____

_____

Unit 12
Review

Ask your teacher for each test and record your grade after you have taken the test.

Part 1 Grade _____

Part 2 Grade _____

Part 3 Grade _____

Part 4 Grade _____

Unit 13

These spelling words contain the sounds of **c** and **g**.

1. geometry
2. gazebo
3. arrange
4. judging
5. guess
6. gorilla
7. region
8. gymnasium
9. August
10. city
11. motorcycle
12. consume
13. excellent
14. cactus
15. customer
16. ceiling
17. cyclone
18. circular

These spelling words contain the hard and soft sounds of **c** and **g**. The hard sound of **c** has the same sound as **k**. The soft sound of **c** has the same sound as **s**. The hard sound of **g** has the same sound you hear in **goat**. The soft sound of **g** has the same sound as **j**.
If a **c** is followed by **e**, **i**, or **y**, it will have the soft sound. If a **g** is followed by an **e**, **i**, or **y**, it will usually have the soft sound. If a **c** is followed by an **a**, **o**, or **u**, it will have the hard sound. If a **g** is followed by an **a**, **o**, or **u**, it will have the hard sound.

Unit 13

1. geometry
2. gazebo
3. arrange
4. judging
5. guess
6. gorilla
7. region
8. gymnasium
9. August
10. city
11. motorcycle
12. consume
13. excellent
14. cactus
15. customer
16. ceiling
17. cyclone
18. circular

A. Write the spelling words which contain the soft sound of **c**.

1. _____ 2. _____

3. _____ 4. _____

5. _____ 6. _____

B. Write the spelling words which contain the soft sound of **g**.

1. _____ 2. _____

3. _____ 4. _____

5. _____

C. Write the spelling words which contain the hard sound of **c**.

1. _____ 2. _____

3. _____ 4. _____

5. _____ 6. _____

D. Write the spelling words which contain the hard sound of **g**.

1. _____ 2. _____

3. _____ 4. _____

E. Write the spelling words which contain both a hard and soft sound of **c**.

1. _____ 2. _____

3. _____

A. Write the spelling words for these dictionary pronunciations.

1. (ə′ rānj) _____

2. (gĕs) _____

3. (sī′ tē) _____

4. (kăk′ təs) _____

5. (sī′ klōn) _____

6. (jəj′ ing) _____

7. (rē′ jən) _____

8. (sēl′ ing) _____

9. (kən′ süm) _____

10. (ô′ gŭst) _____

B. Write these words in syllables. Use your spelling glossary.

1. geometry _____

2. gorilla _____

3. motorcycle _____

4. excellent _____

5. gazebo _____

6. gymnasium _____

7. circular _____

8. customer _____

Write the word that fits each definition.

1. _____ a free standing roofed building that is open on the sides

2. _____ room made for physical exercise

3. _____ a large part of the earth's surface

4. _____ making a decision about an issue

5. _____ a spiny, fleshy stemmed plant with no leaves

6. _____ a very violent wind storm

7. _____ to use up; destroy

8. _____ a large important town

9. _____ a branch of math that measures lines and angles

10. _____ a person who buys

11. _____ to put things in a special order

12. _____ to form an opinion without knowing exactly

13. _____ a very large ape

14. _____ the eighth month of the year

15. _____ a bike that is run by a motor

16. _____ extremely good

17. _____ the inside top covering of a room

18. _____ round like a circle

Write the spelling words three times.

1. geometry _____ _____

   _____

2. gazebo _____ _____

   _____

3. arrange _____ _____

   _____

4. judging _____ _____

   _____

5. guess _____ _____

   _____

6. gorilla _____ _____

   _____

7. region _____ _____

   _____

8. gymnasium _____ _____

   _____

9. August _____ _____

   _____

10. city _____ _____

_____

11. motorcycle_____ _____

_____

12. consume_____ _____

_____

13. excellent _____ _____

_____

14. cactus _____ _____

_____

15. customer _____ _____

_____

16. ceiling _____ _____

_____

17. cyclone_____ _____

_____

18. circular _____ _____

_____

Unit 14

These spelling words contain the **z** or **zh** sound.

1. lose
2. reserve
3. pleasant
4. tease
5. visible
6. sneeze
7. cheese
8. miserable
9. zone
10. scissors
11. busiest
12. exercise
13. pleasure
14. measure
15. usual
16. chosen
17. magazine
18. treasure

The **z** or the **zh** sound can be made by the letter **z** as in **zoo**, or by the letter **s** as in **cheese**. The **zh** sound can be made by the letter **s** as in **measure**.

Unit 14

1. lose
2. reserve
3. pleasant
4. tease
5. visible
6. sneeze
7. cheese
8. miserable
9. zone
10. scissors
11. busiest
12. exercise
13. pleasure
14. measure
15. usual
16. chosen
17. magazine
18. treasure

A. Write the spelling words that have the **z** sound spelled by the letter **s**.

1. _____   2. _____
3. _____   4. _____
5. _____   6. _____
7. _____   8. _____
9. _____   10. _____
11. _____

B. Write the spelling words that have the **z** sound spelled by the letter **z**.

1. _____   2. _____
3. _____

C. Write the spelling words that have the **zh** sound spelled by the letter **s**.

1. _____   2. _____
3. _____   4. _____

D. Write the three syllable spelling words.

1. _____   2. _____
3. _____   4. _____
5. _____

E. Write the four syllable spelling word.

_____

A. Write the spelling word for each dictionary pronunciation.

1. (mĭz′ ər ə bəl) _____

2. (rĭ zėrv′) _____

3. (trĕzh′ ər) _____

4. (ĕk′ sər sīz) _____

5. (plĕz′ ənt) _____

6. (sĭz′ ərz) _____

B. Underline the spelling word in each sentence. Write its part of speech.

1. I love to eat cheese with crackers. _____

2. Who is the busiest teacher in the school? _____

3. I do not like to lose my shoes. _____

4. I do not read the magazine very much at all. _____

5. Today is a usual fall day. _____

6. In which zone do you live? _____

C. Write these words in alphabetical order.

tease   visible   sneeze   chosen   pleasure   measure

1. _____   4. _____

2. _____   5. _____

3. _____   6. _____

Fill in the blanks with spelling words. You will need to add **s** to two words.

1. I have _____ to bake chicken for supper.

2. Frankie's headaches caused him to be _____.

3. The day after Thanksgiving is the _____ shopping day of the year for some stores.

4. Donna used _____ to cut David's hair.

5. Many brothers like to _____ their sisters.

6. Cover your nose when you _____.

7. Be sure to not _____ your homework.

8. Kentucky had three _____ with different area codes.

9. It appeared that Mr. Conrad was looking for buried _____.

10. It was a _____ to work with Patrick.

11. I like to eat _____.

12. When looking for a job, be sure to have a _____ smile.

13. Jogging is a good _____.

14. Did you _____ to see how wide the table is?

15. Please _____ the book for me at the library.

16. From where I sat, the cobweb was still _____.

17. I do not want a bunch of _____ to clutter my table.

18. Is this weather _____ for fall?

Write the spelling words three times.

1. lose _____ _____

   _____

2. reserve _____ _____

   _____

3. pleasant _____ _____

   _____

4. tease _____ _____

   _____

5. visible _____ _____

   _____

6. sneeze _____ _____

   _____

7. cheese _____ _____

   _____

8. miserable _____ _____

   _____

9. zone _____ _____

   _____

10. scissors _____ _____

_____

11. busiest _____ _____

_____

12. exercise _____ _____

_____

13. pleasure _____ _____

_____

14. measure _____ _____

_____

15. usual _____ _____

_____

16. chosen _____ _____

_____

17. magazine _____ _____

_____

18. treasure _____ _____

_____

Unit 15

These spelling words contain the **ch** sound as in **child** or the **sh** sound as in **she**.

1. pasture
2. capture
3. natural
4. ancient
5. station
6. special
7. chopper
8. ocean
9. benches
10. champion
11. facial
12. patch
13. adventure
14. finish
15. channel
16. fraction
17. patiently
18. shiver

The **ch** sound can be made by the letters **tch** as in **hatch**, or by the letters **ch** as in **chores**. It can also be made by the letters **tu** as in **pasture**. The **sh** sound can be made by the letters **sh** as in **shell**, or by the letters **ti** as in **fiction**. It can also be made by the letters **ci** as in **ancient**, or by the letters **ce** as in **ocean**.

Unit 15

1. pasture
2. capture
3. natural
4. ancient
5. station
6. special
7. chopper
8. ocean
9. benches
10. champion
11. facial
12. patch
13. adventure
14. finish
15. channel
16. fraction
17. patiently
18. shiver

A. Write the spelling words in which the **ch** sound is spelled by the letters **ch** or **tch**.

1. _____ 2. _____

3. _____ 4. _____

5. _____

B. Write the spelling words in which the letters **tu** spell the **ch** sound.

1. _____ 2. _____

3. _____ 4. _____

C. Write the spelling words in which the letters **ci** spell the **sh** sound.

1. _____ 2. _____

3. _____

D. Write the spelling words in which the letters **ti** spell the **sh** sound.

1. _____ 2. _____

3. _____

E. Write the spelling word in which the letters **ce** spell the **sh** sound.

_____

F. Write the spelling words in which the **sh** sound is spellsed with an **sh**.

1. _____ 2. _____

G. Write the spelling words that have double consonants.

1. _____ 2. _____

A. One word in each set is misspelled. Write the word correctly.

1. benches, natcheral, patch _____

2. choper, ocean, fraction _____

3. channel, station, pashently _____

4. paschur, facial, shiver _____

5. finish, ancient, speceal _____

6. champeon, capture, adventure _____

B. Write these words in syllables.

1. capture _____

2. facial _____

3. ocean _____

4. benches _____

C. Write these words in alphabetical order.

| capture | ancient | station | patch |
| adventure | channel | fraction | shiver |

1. _____ 5. _____

2. _____ 6. _____

3. _____ 7. _____

4. _____ 8. _____

Write the word that fits each definition.

1. _____ something that chops

2. _____ to complete

3. _____ a grassy field where cattle can feed

4. _____ produced by nature

5. _____ with calmness to handle difficulties

6. _____ a small piece of cloth used for mending

7. _____ the winner

8. _____ a stopping place for trains and buses

9. _____ of the face; for the face

10. _____ to take by force or skill

11. _____ a large body of salt water

12. _____ very old

13. _____ of a particular kind; not general

14. _____ long seats made of wood

15. _____ an exciting happening

16. _____ one part of a whole

17. _____ to shake with cold or fear

18. _____ a path cut by water

Write the spelling words three times.

1. pasture _____ _____

   _____

2. capture _____ _____

   _____

3. natural _____ _____

   _____

4. ancient _____ _____

   _____

5. station _____ _____

   _____

6. special _____ _____

   _____

7. chopper _____ _____

   _____

8. ocean _____ _____

   _____

9. benches _____ _____

   _____

10. champion _____ _____
    _____

11. facial _____ _____
    _____

12. patch _____ _____
    _____

13. adventure _____ _____
    _____

14. finish _____ _____
    _____

15. channel _____ _____
    _____

16. fraction _____ _____
    _____

17. patiently _____ _____
    _____

18. shiver _____ _____
    _____

Unit 16

These spelling words contain the schwa sound.

1. around
2. student
3. afar
4. colony
5. ribbon
6. distance
7. cousin
8. adopt
9. elementary
10. adobe
11. necessary
12. finally
13. beautiful
14. certainly
15. barrel
16. talent
17. cafeteria
18. refrigerator

The schwa sound can be made by the vowels, **a**, **e**, **i**, **o**, and **u**. The schwa sound is heard in the unaccented syllables in a word. In the dictionary pronunciation key the schwa is represented with the symbol ə.

Unit 16

1. around
2. student
3. afar
4. colony
5. ribbon
6. distance
7. cousin
8. adopt
9. elementary
10. adobe
11. necessary
12. finally
13. beautiful
14. certainly
15. barrel
16. talent
17. cafeteria
18. refrigerator

A. Write the spelling words which contain the **schwa** sound spelled by the letter **a** or by the letters **ai**.

1. _____ 2. _____

3. _____ 4. _____

5. _____ 6. _____

7. _____ 8. _____

9. _____

B. Write the spelling words which contain the **schwa** sound spelled by the letter **e**.

1. _____ 2. _____

3. _____ 4. _____

5. _____ 6. _____

7. _____

C. Write the spelling words which contain the **schwa** sound spelled by the letter **i**.

1. _____ 2. _____

D. Write the spelling words which contain the **schwa** sound spelled by the letter **o**.

1. _____ 2. _____

E. Write the spelling word in which one **schwa** sound is spelled by the letter **u**.

_____

A. Write these words in syllables.

1. refrigerator _____

2. elementary _____

3. cafeteria _____

4. necessary _____

5. colony _____

6. certainly _____

7. finally _____

8. beautiful _____

B. One word in each set is misspelled. Write the word correctly.

1. student, arownd, barrel _____

2. tolent, adobe, distance _____

3. afar, ribbon, cusin, _____

4. adopt, barrel, studant _____

C. Find these words in your spelling glossary. Write its part of speech.

1. afar _____ 2. ribbon _____

3. adopt _____ 4. barrel _____

5. distance _____ 6. adobe _____

A. Complete the sentences with spelling words.

1. Donna's banquet dress was _____.

2. I went to Fairdale _____ School.

3. We could burn garbage in a _____.

4. Milk should be kept in a _____.

5. I wanted to decorate some dresses with the red _____.

6. Levi was not a _____ in our school.

7. Kevin and Patti thought they might _____ a child.

8. We could eat in the school _____.

9. I _____ finished the quilt.

10. Tony had a wonderful _____ for playing the piano.

B. Write the word that fits each definition.

1. _____ in a circle; about

2. _____ the child of one's aunt or uncle

3. _____ far away

4. _____ needed

5. _____ a group of people that settle together

6. _____ the space between two things

7. _____ without a doubt

8. _____ bricks made from sun-dried clay

Write the spelling words three times.

1. around

2. student

3. afar

4. colony

5. ribbon

6. distance

7. cousin

8. adopt

9. elementary

10. adobe _____ _____

    _____

11. necessary _____ _____

    _____

12. finally _____ _____

    _____

13. beautiful _____ _____

    _____

14. certainly _____ _____

    _____

15. barrel _____ _____

    _____

16. talent _____ _____

    _____

17. cafeteria _____ _____

    _____

18. refrigerator _____

    _____

    _____

Unit 17

These spelling words have a short **u** or a long **u** sound.

1. glove
2. none
3. wonder
4. uniform
5. jumble
6. young
7. community
8. dump
9. human
10. shove
11. cuff
12. excused
13. future
14. company
15. tongue
16. couple
17. budget
18. avenue

The short **u** sound in these words can be spelled with a **u** as in **cup**. It can also be spelled with **o** as in **none** or **ou** as in **young**.
The long **u** sound can be spelled with **u** at the end of an open syllable. It can also be spelled by the **u** + **consonant** + **e** pattern as in **abuse**. Another way is by the letters **ue** as in **revenue**.

Unit 17

1. glove
2. none
3. wonder
4. uniform
5. jumble
6. young
7. community
8. dump
9. human
10. shove
11. cuff
12. excused
13. future
14. company
15. tongue
16. couple
17. budget
18. avenue

A. Write the spelling words which have the long **u** sound at the end of an open syllable.

1. _____   2. _____

3. _____   4. _____

B. Write the spelling words which have the short **u** sound spelled by the letter **u**.

1. _____   2. _____

3. _____   4. _____

C. Write the spelling words which have the short **u** sound spelled by the letter **o**.

1. _____   2. _____

3. _____   4. _____

5. _____   6. _____

D. Write the spelling words which have the short **u** sound spelled by the letters **ou**.

1. _____   2. _____

E. Write the spelling word that has the long **u** sound spelled by the **u + consonant + e** pattern.

_____

F. Write the spelling word that has the long **u** sound spelled by the letters **ue**.

_____

G. Write the four syllable spelling word.

_____

A. Write the spelling word for each dictionary pronunciation.

1. (jŭm′ bəl) _____

2. (glŭv) _____ 3. (yŭng) _____

4. (bŭj′ ĭt) _____ 5. (nŭn) _____

6. (kŭf) _____ 7. (shŭv) _____

8. (dŭmp) _____ 9. (tŭng) _____

10. (kŭp′ əl) _____

11. (hū′ mən) _____

12. (wŭn′ dər) _____

13. (ĕk skūzd′) _____

14. (fū′ chər) _____

B. Write these words in syllables.

1. uniform _____

2. community _____

3. company _____

4. avenue _____

C. Write these words in alphabetical order.
  community   cuff   company   couple

1. _____ 2. _____

3. _____ 4. _____

Fill in the blanks with spelling words.

1. I like our school _____ for girls to be jumpers.

2. Not many children were gathering candy on Halloween in our _____.

3. Many people save money for their _____.

4. A _____ truck poured rocks on our driveway.

5. Make sure to include money in your _____ for a car.

6. The _____ of my blouse was stained.

7. I lived on Morgan _____ for almost eight years.

8. I _____ what caused the wreck.

9. You should never _____ another person.

10. Because James was sick, his absence could be _____.

11. Donna was very _____ the first time I took her shopping.

12. We had company for a _____ of days.

13. Was a finger cut on the blue _____ ?

14. It is not pleasant to accidentally bite your _____.

15. Kevin worked for a plumbing _____.

16. To have _____, means you don't have any.

17. Don't shake the container and _____ the blocks.

18. We are all _____ and can make mistakes.

Write the spelling words three times.

1. glove _____ _____

   _____

2. none _____ _____

   _____

3. wonder_____ _____

   _____

4. uniform _____ _____

   _____

5. jumble _____ _____

   _____

6. young _____ _____

   _____

7. community _____ _____

   _____

8. dump _____ _____

   _____

9. human _____ _____

   _____

10. shove _____ _____

_____

11. cuff _____ _____

_____

12. excused _____ _____

_____

13. future _____ _____

_____

14. company _____ _____

_____

15. tongue _____ _____

_____

16. couple _____ _____

_____

17. budget _____ _____

_____

18. avenue _____ _____

_____

Unit 18
Review

Ask your teacher for each test and record your grade after you have taken the test.

Part 1 Grade _____

Part 2 Grade _____

Part 3 Grade _____

Part 4 Grade _____

Unit 19

These spelling words have prefixes.

1. disapprove
2. disagree
3. discomfort
4. misdirect
5. misbehave
6. misunderstand
7. unkind
8. uncover
9. unbeatable
10. irregular
11. irreplaceable
12. incapable
13. inactive
14. impossible
15. impure
16. dishonor
17. misspell
18. discourtesy

These spelling words have the prefixes **dis**, **mis**, **un**, **ir**, **in**, and **im**. These prefixes often mean "not," "the opposite of," or "wrong." Adding these prefixes to a word changes the word's meaning to the opposite.

Unit 19

1. disapprove
2. disagree
3. discomfort
4. misdirect
5. misbehave
6. misunderstand
7. unkind
8. uncover
9. unbeatable
10. irregular
11. irreplaceable
12. incapable
13. inactive
14. impossible
15. impure
16. dishonor
17. misspell
18. discourtesy

A. Write the spelling words that have the prefix **dis**.

1. _____ 2. _____

3. _____ 4. _____

5. _____

B. Write the spelling words that have the prefix **mis**.

1. _____ 2. _____

3. _____ 4. _____

C. Write the spelling words that have the prefix **un**.

1. _____ 2. _____

3. _____

D. Write the spelling words that have the prefix **ir**.

1. _____ 2. _____

E. Write the spelling words that have the prefix **in**.

1. _____ 2. _____

F. Write the spelling words that have the prefix **im**.

1. _____ 2. _____

G. Write the spelling word that has five syllables.

_____

A. Write these words in alphabetical order.

dishonor   disagree   discourtesy   disapprove   discomfort

1. _____   4. _____

2. _____   5. _____

3. _____

B. Find each of these words in your spelling glossary. Write its part of speech.

1. misspell _____   2. unkind _____

3. misdirect _____   4. uncover _____

5. misbehave _____   6. impure _____

7. discourtesy _____   8. discomfort _____

C. Write each of these words in syllables using hyphens. Use your spelling glossary.

1. impossible _____

2. incapable _____

3. irreplaceable _____

4. irregular _____

5. misunderstand _____

6. unbeatable _____

7. inactive _____

A. Use spelling words to complete the paragraph. The first letter is given for each one.

I think children should not (1) m_____. I (2) d_____ of letting them always have what they want. Do not (3) m_____ me. I (4) d_____ with beating a child, but a spanking should cause some (5) d_____. Children need to be corrected if they (6) d_____ their parents or treat others in an (7) u_____ way. It is not (8) i_____ to train children in the right way.

B. Fill in the spelling word that matches each definition.

1. _____ to give wrong directions
2. _____ to reveal something that is covered
3. _____ something that can not be replaced
4. _____ to spell incorrectly
5. _____ the best; can not be beaten
6. _____ impoliteness
7. _____ unusual; not regular
8. _____ not pure
9. _____ not able to do something
10. _____ not active

Write the spelling words three times.

1. disapprove _____ _____

   _____

2. disagree _____ _____

   _____

3. discomfort _____ _____

   _____

4. misdirect _____ _____

   _____

5. misbehave _____ _____

   _____

6. misunderstand _____

   _____

   _____

7. unkind _____ _____

   _____

8. uncover _____ _____

   _____

9. unbeatable _____ _____

   _____

10. irregular _____ _____

_____

11. irreplaceable _____

_____

_____

12. incapable _____ _____

_____

13. inactive _____ _____

_____

14. impossible _____

_____

_____

15. impure _____ _____

_____

16. dishonor _____ _____

_____

17. misspell _____ _____

_____

18. discourtesy _____

_____

_____

Unit 20

These spelling words have prefixes.

1. nonstop
2. nonliving
3. enlarge
4. entangle
5. enrich
6. malnourished
7. maltreat
8. nonsense
9. nonresident
10. precook
11. prejudge
12. prohibit
13. procrastinate
14. return
15. recall
16. prepaid
17. retrace
18. rewrite

These spelling words have the prefixes **non**, **en**, **mal**, **pre**, **pro**, and **re**. The prefix **non** means "**not**." The prefix **en** means **"cause to be"** or **"make."** The prefix **mal** usually means "**bad**" or "**badly**." The prefixes **pre** and **pro** usually mean "**before**." **Pro** can also mean "**forward**." **Re** is a prefix that means "**again**" or "**back**."

Unit 20

1. nonstop
2. nonliving
3. enlarge
4. entangle
5. enrich
6. malnourished
7. maltreat
8. nonsense
9. nonresident
10. precook
11. prejudge
12. prohibit
13. procrastinate
14. return
15. recall
16. prepaid
17. retrace
18. rewrite

A. Write the spelling words that have the prefix **non**.

1. _____ 2. _____

3. _____ 4. _____

B. Write the spelling words that have the prefix **en**.

1. _____ 2. _____

3. _____

C. Write the spelling words that have the prefix **mal**.

1. _____ 2. _____

D. Write the spelling words that have the prefix **pre**.

1. _____ 2. _____

3. _____

E. Write the spelling words that have the prefix **pro**.

1. _____ 2. _____

F. Write the spelling words that have the prefix **re**.

1. _____ 2. _____

3. _____ 4. _____

G. Write the spelling words that have four syllables.

1. _____

2. _____

A. Write the spelling word for each dictionary pronunciation.

1. (ĕn tăng′ gəl) _____

2. (ĕn rĭch′) _____

3. (măl nėr′ ĭshd) _____

4. (măl trēt′) _____

5. (ĕn lärj′)) _____

B. Write these words in syllables. Use your spelling glossary.

1. procrastinate _____

2. nonresident _____

3. nonliving _____

4. prohibit _____

C. One word in each set is misspelled. Write the word correctly.

1. precook, nonsence, recall _____

2. rerite, prepaid, nonstop _____

3. return, prejudge, retrase _____

4. nonliving, retern, maltreat _____

5. percook, prohibit, enrich _____

6. rewrite, malnourished, nunstop _____

7. entangle, nonresident, recal _____

8. prejudje, procrastinate, enrich _____

9. nonliving, entangle, prepayd _____

Write the word that fits each definition.

1. _____ not alive
2. _____ to cook before it is needed
3. _____ not enough nutrition
4. _____ one who does not live in a certain area
5. _____ to write again
6. _____ foolishness
7. _____ to make larger
8. _____ to forbid by law or authority
9. _____ to treat roughly or cruelly
10. _____ to put off something that should be done
11. _____ go back to something
12. _____ without stopping
13. _____ get twisted or caught
14. _____ to judge before fully hearing the story
15. _____ a summons to return
16. _____ to make rich
17. _____ to pay in advance
18. _____ to go over again or in a reverse direction

Write the spelling words three times.

1. nonstop _____ _____

   _____

2. nonliving _____ _____

   _____

3. enlarge _____ _____

   _____

4. entangle _____ _____

   _____

5. enrich _____ _____

   _____

6. malnourished _____

   _____

   _____

7. maltreat _____ _____

   _____

8. nonsense _____ _____

   _____

9. nonresident _____ _____

   _____

10. precook _____ _____

_____

11. prejudge _____ _____

_____

12. prohibit _____ _____

_____

13. procrastinate _____

_____

_____

14. return _____ _____

_____

15. recall _____ _____

_____

16. prepaid _____ _____

_____

17. retrace _____ _____

_____

18. rewrite _____ _____

_____

Unit 21

These spelling words have prefixes.

1. export
2. excuse
3. exchange
4. co-author
5. co-directors
6. cooperate
7. combine
8. compile
9. compel
10. conspire
11. conceal
12. conduct
13. subway
14. submarine
15. submerge
16. midweek
17. midnight
18. midstream

These spelling words have the prefixes **ex**, **co**, **con**, **com**, **sub**, and **mid**. The prefix **ex** means "**out of**" or "**from**." The prefixes **co, con,** and **com** mean **"with"** or **"together."** The prefix **sub** means "**under**," "**below**," or "**not quite**." The prefix **mid** means "**middle part**."

Unit 21

1. export
2. excuse
3. exchange
4. co-author
5. co-directors
6. cooperate
7. combine
8. compile
9. compel
10. conspire
11. conceal
12. conduct
13. subway
14. submarine
15. submerge
16. midweek
17. midnight
18. midstream

A. Write the spelling words that have the prefix **co**.

1. _____ 2. _____

3. _____

B. Write the spelling words that have the prefix **ex**.

1. _____ 2. _____

3. _____

C. Write the spelling words that have the prefix **mid**.

1. _____ 2. _____

3. _____

D. Write the spelling words that have the prefix **com**.

1. _____ 2. _____

3. _____

E. Write the spelling words that have the prefix **sub**.

1. _____ 2. _____

3. _____

F. Write the spelling words that have the prefix **con**.

1. _____ 2. _____

3. _____

G. Write the spelling word that describes a kind of ship.

_____

A. Write the spelling word that is a synonym for each word.

1. forgive _____ 2. join _____

3. force _____ 4. hide _____

5. lead _____

B. Write these words in syllables. Use your spelling glossary.

1. co-directors _____

2. cooperate _____

3. submarine _____

4. co-author _____

C. Write the spelling word which came from these base or root words.

1. change _____

2. stream _____

3. pile _____

4. way _____

5. spire _____

6. night _____

7. port _____

8. merge _____

9. week _____

Complete the sentences with spelling words.

1. We can _____ work and play to make learning fun.

2. The water may be deeper at _____.

3. Many people ride the _____ in New York.

4. Please say "_____ me," if you burp.

5. I would like to have a _____ when writing this book.

6. We give voters a shield so they can _____ their vote.

7. It was after _____ when I went to bed.

8. Does America _____ goods to other countries?

9. I wish I could _____ Lee to stay out of trouble.

10. Our _____ service is on Wednesday.

11. We could _____ presents at a Christmas dinner.

12. I wanted the students to _____ with me during play practice.

13. We did not have a tour guide to _____ us.

14. David was going to _____ Jimmy under the water.

15. Please _____ all your daily work on the shelf.

16. Was the Lusitania a _____?

17. Please do not _____ against me to have a bad day.

18. Were there two _____ for the film?

Write the spelling words three times.

1. export _____ _____

   _____

2. excuse _____ _____

   _____

3. exchange _____ _____

   _____

4. co-author _____ _____

   _____

5. co-directors _____

   _____

   _____

6. cooperate _____ _____

   _____

7. combine _____ _____

   _____

8. compile _____ _____

   _____

9. compel _____ _____

   _____

10. conspire _____ _____

_____

11. conceal _____ _____

_____

12. conduct _____ _____

_____

13. subway _____ _____

_____

14. submarine _____

_____

_____

15. submerge _____ _____

_____

16. midweek _____ _____

_____

17. midnight _____ _____

_____

18. midstream _____

_____

_____

Unit 22

These spelling words have suffixes.

1. teacher
2. baker
3. actor
4. projector
5. novelist
6. collector
7. golden
8. scientist
9. engineer
10. employee
11. auctioneer
12. absentee
13. harden
14. thicken
15. servant
16. assistant
17. backward
18. skyward

These spelling words have the suffixes **er, or, ist, eer, ee, en, ant,** and **ward**. The suffixes **er** and **or** can change a verb into a noun that means **"someone who does something"** or **"a thing that can do something."** The suffix **ist**, changes a noun that means "a thing" into a noun that means **"someone who does something."** The suffix **ward** means **"in the direction of."** The suffix **en** means **"to make,"** or **"become."** The suffixes **eer, ee,** and **ant** usually mean **"someone who."**

Unit 22

1. teacher
2. baker
3. actor
4. projector
5. novelist
6. collector
7. golden
8. scientist
9. engineer
10. employee
11. auctioneer
12. absentee
13. harden
14. thicken
15. servant
16. assistant
17. backward
18. skyward

A. Write the spelling words that have the suffix **er**.

1. _____ 2. _____

B. Write the spelling words that have the suffix **or**.

1. _____ 2. _____

3. _____

C. Write the spelling words that have the suffix **ist**.

1. _____ 2. _____

D. Write the spelling words that have the suffix **eer**.

1. _____ 2. _____

E. Write the spelling words that have the suffix **ee**.

1. _____ 2. _____

F. Write the spelling words that have the suffix **en**.

1. _____ 2. _____

3. _____

G. Write the spelling words that have the suffix **ant**.

1. _____ 2. _____

H. Write the spelling words that have the suffix **ward**.

1. _____ 2. _____

A. Write the two-syllable spelling words.

1. _____ 2. _____

3. _____ 4. _____

5. _____ 6. _____

7. _____ 8. _____

9. _____

B. Write the three-syllable spelling words.

1. _____ 2. _____

3. _____ 4. _____

5. _____ 6. _____

7. _____ 8. _____

9. _____

C. Write the spelling words which do not refer to people.

1. _____ 2. _____

3. _____ 4. _____

5. _____ 6. _____

D. Find these words in your spelling glossary. Write its part of speech.

1. thicken _____ 2. backward _____

3. absentee _____ 4. golden _____

Write the word that fits each definition.

1. _____ in the direction of the sky

2. _____ having a bright yellow color

3. _____ a thing that projects

4. _____ a person who serves

5. _____ a person who writes novels

6. _____ a person who bakes

7. _____ one who studies laws of nature

8. _____ to make thick

9. _____ one who is not present

10. _____ one who entertains others by acting

11. _____ one who is employed by a company

12. _____ a person who helps others learn

13. _____ a person who helps a teacher

14. _____ a designer or builder of engines

15. _____ toward the back

16. _____ one who collects many of a certain thing

17. _____ a person who conducts an auction

18. _____ to make more firm

Write the spelling words three times.

1. teacher _____ _____

   _____

2. baker _____ _____

   _____

3. actor _____ _____

   _____

4. projector _____ _____

   _____

5. novelist _____ _____

   _____

6. collector _____ _____

   _____

7. golden _____ _____

   _____

8. scientist _____ _____

   _____

9. engineer _____ _____

   _____

10. employee _____ _____

_____

11. auctioneer _____ _____

_____

12. absentee _____ _____

_____

13. harden _____ _____

_____

14. thicken _____ _____

_____

15. servant _____ _____

_____

16. assistant _____ _____

_____

17. backward _____ _____

_____

18. skyward _____ _____

_____

Unit 23

These spelling words have suffixes.

1. dangerous
2. government
3. courageous
4. appointment
5. washable
6. reversible
7. dependable
8. reducible
9. importance
10. acceptance
11. impressive
12. creative
13. reality
14. legality
15. confidence
16. dependence
17. marvelous
18. continuous

These spelling words have the suffixes **ous, ment, able, ible, ance, ity, ence,** and **ive**. The suffix **ous** means "**being full of.**" The suffix **ment,** means "**the state or condition of being.**" The suffixes **able** and **ible** mean "**able to be**" or "**full of.**" The suffixes **ance, ence**, and **ity** usually mean "**the quality,**" or "**state of being.**" The suffix **ive** usually means "**likely to.**" or "**having to do with.**"

Unit 23

1. dangerous
2. government
3. courageous
4. appointment
5. washable
6. reversible
7. dependable
8. reducible
9. importance
10. acceptance
11. impressive
12. creative
13. reality
14. legality
15. confidence
16. dependence
17. marvelous
18. continuous

A. Write the spelling words that have the suffix **ous**.

1. _____ 2. _____

3. _____ 4. _____

B. Write the spelling words that have the suffix **ment**.

1. _____ 2. _____

C. Write the spelling words that have the suffix **able**.

1. _____ 2. _____

D. Write the spelling words that have the suffix **ible**.

1. _____ 2. _____

E. Write the spelling words that have the suffix **ance**.

1. _____ 2. _____

F. Write the spelling words that have the suffix **ive**.

1. _____ 2. _____

G. Write the spelling words that have the suffix **ity**.

1. _____ 2. _____

H. Write the spelling words that have the suffix **ence**.

1. _____ 2. _____

A. Write a spelling word that is a synonym for each word.

1. risky _____

2. brave _____

3. wonderful _____

4. boldness _____

5. constant _____

6. inventive _____

B. Write the spelling word for each dictionary pronunciation.

1. (rĭ oul′ ĭ tē) _____

2. (gŭv′ ərn mənt) _____

3. (dĭ pĕn′ dəns) _____

4. (ĭm pôr′ təns) _____

5. (ăk sĕp′ təns) _____

6. (ə point′ mənt) _____

C. Write the spelling word that matches each definition.

1. _____ lawful

2. _____ able to be reduced

3. _____ able to be reversed

4. _____ able to impress the mind

5. _____ trustworthy

6. _____ able to be washed

Complete the sentences with spelling words.

1. A _____ person can make many things.

2. It is a _____ thing to meet a bear in the woods.

3. If you trust someone, then you have _____ in them, and you consider them to be a _____ person.

4. Matthew's grade on his algebra test was _____.

5. Patti had a doctor's _____.

6. I washed the coat since it was _____.

7. Since the picture can be made smaller, it is _____.

8. His _____ talking was annoying to others.

9. Brian was very _____ to save John from drowning.

10. Jesus did a _____ thing when He healed a blind man.

11. Is it of great _____ to own a diamond ring?

12. I would like to work for the _____; I could learn the _____ of some things.

13. I was happy to learn their _____ of my offer.

14. What is the _____ of seeing a dinosaur on your porch?

15. My _____ on my husband's strength is obvious.

16. The sweater was different on the inside, so it is not _____.

Write the spelling words three times.

1. dangerous _____ _____

   _____

2. government _____ _____

   _____

3. courageous _____ _____

   _____

4. appointment _____

   _____

   _____

5. washable _____ _____

   _____

6. reversible _____ _____

   _____

7. dependable _____ _____

   _____

8. reducible _____ _____

   _____

9. importance _____ _____

   _____

10. acceptance _____

    _____

    _____

11. impressive _____

    _____

    _____

12. creative _____ _____

    _____

13. reality _____ _____

    _____

14. legality _____ _____

    _____

15. confidence _____ _____

    _____

16. dependence _____ _____

    _____

17. marvelous _____ _____

    _____

18. continuous _____

    _____

    _____

Unit 24
Review

Ask your teacher for each test and record your grade after you have taken the test.

Part 1 Grade _____

Part 2 Grade _____

Part 3 Grade _____

Part 4 Grade _____

Unit 25

These spelling words contain the consonant digraph **ch**.

1. Chicago
2. cheering
3. purchase
4. brochure
5. check
6. champion
7. coach
8. change
9. choose
10. attach
11. chauffeur
12. charity
13. chandelier
14. chagrin
15. chamber
16. chaise
17. church
18. chute

These spelling words contain the consonant digraph **ch**. The **ch** can make the sound you hear in **church**, or it can sound like the **sh** in **show**.

Unit 25

1. Chicago
2. cheering
3. purchase
4. brochure
5. check
6. champion
7. coach
8. change
9. choose
10. attach
11. chauffeur
12. charity
13. chandelier
14. chagrin
15. chamber
16. chaise
17. church
18. chute

A. Write the spelling words which have the **ch** sound you hear in **choice**.

1. _____ 2. _____

3. _____ 4. _____

5. _____ 6. _____

7. _____ 8. _____

9. _____ 10. _____

11. _____

B. Write the spelling words which have the **sh** sound spelled with a **ch**.

1. _____ 2. _____

3. _____ 4. _____

5. _____ 6. _____

7. _____

C. Write the three-syllable spelling words.

1. _____ 2. _____

3. _____ 4. _____

D. Write the one-syllable spelling words.

1. _____ 2. _____

3. _____ 4. _____

5. _____ 6. _____

7. _____

A. Write the word for each dictionary pronunciation.

1. (chĕk) _____ 2. (shāz) _____

3. (cōch) _____ 4. (shüt) _____

5. (chānj) _____ 6. (chûrch) _____

7. (shĭ kŏ′ gō) _____

8. (pûr′ chĭs) _____

9. (ə tăch′) _____

10. (chãr′ ĭ tē) _____

11. (shə grĭn′) _____

12. (chēr′ ĭng) _____

13. (brō shủr′) _____

14. (chăm′ pĭ ən) _____

15. (chüz) _____

16. (shō′ fər) _____

17. (shăn′ də lĭr) _____

18. (chām′ bėr) _____

B. Underline the spelling word in each sentence. Write its part of speech.

1. Did you read the brochure? _____

2. Please check the correct box. _____

3. Goliath thought he was a champion. _____

4. Choose you this day whom you will serve. _____

150

Write the word that fits each definition.

1. _____ a booklet containing advertising material

2. _____ a large four-wheeled horse-drawn carriage

3. _____ a building for public worship

4. _____ annoyance caused by failure; disappointment

5. _____ to obtain by paying money

6. _____ goodwill toward or love of humanity

7. _____ a large city in Illinois

8. _____ to bind together

9. _____ a warrior; a fighter

10. _____ to select freely

11. _____ a person employed to drive an automobile

12. _____ two-wheeled horse drawn carriage with a folding top

13. _____ an inclined passage for things

14. _____ to make or become different

15. _____ the act of giving hope or comfort

16. _____ a branched lighting fixture suspended from the ceiling

17. _____ a mark placed beside an item

18. _____ a judge's consultation room

Write the spelling words three times.

1. Chicago _____ _____

   _____

2. cheering _____ _____

   _____

3. purchase _____ _____

   _____

4. brochure _____ _____

   _____

5. check _____ _____

   _____

6. champion _____ _____

   _____

7. coach _____ _____

   _____

8. change _____ _____

   _____

9. choose _____ _____

   _____

10. attach _____ _____

_____

11. chauffeur _____ _____

_____

12. charity _____ _____

_____

13. chandelier _____

_____

_____

14. chagrin _____ _____

_____

15. chamber _____ _____

_____

16. chaise _____ _____

_____

17. church _____ _____

_____

18. chute _____ _____

_____

Unit 26

These spelling words contain the consonant digraph **ch**.

1. chorus
2. character
3. anchor
4. chaos
5. chameleon
6. chaff
7. chance
8. chemical
9. chart
10. chateau
11. chocolate
12. chef
13. chivalry
14. chemist
15. Christ
16. cholera
17. Christmas
18. architect

These spelling words contain the consonant digraph **ch**. The **ch** can make the **ch** sound as in **church**, the **sh** sound as in **chef**, or the **k** sound as in **chord**.

Unit 26

1. chorus
2. character
3. anchor
4. chaos
5. chameleon
6. chaff
7. chance
8. chemical
9. chart
10. chateau
11. chocolate
12. chef
13. chivalry
14. chemist
15. Christ
16. cholera
17. Christmas
18. architect

A. Write the spelling words which have the **ch** sound you hear in **choose**.

1. _____ 2. _____

3. _____ 4. _____

B. Write the spelling words which have the **sh** sound spelled with a **ch**.

1. _____ 2. _____

3. _____

C. Write the spelling words which have the **k** sound spelled with a **ch**.

1. _____ 2. _____

3. _____ 4. _____

5. _____ 6. _____

7. _____ 8. _____

9. _____ 10. _____

11. _____

D. Write the spelling word that names a famous person.

_____

E. Write the spelling word that names a holiday.

_____

F. Write the spelling word that has double consonants.

_____

A. Write the spelling word for each dictionary pronunciation.

1. (chăf) _____ 2. (krīst) _____

3. (kā′ ŏs) _____ 4. (chăns) _____

5. (chärt) _____ 6. (kô′ rəs) _____

7. (ăng′ kər) _____ 8. (shĕf) _____

9. (shĭv′ əl rē) _____

10. (är′ kə tĕkt) _____

11. (kŏl′ ər ə) _____

12. (shă tō′) _____

13. (chŏk′ ə lĭt) _____

14. (kãr′ ĭk tər) _____

15. (krĭs′ məs) _____

16. (kə mēl′ yən) _____

17. (kĕm′ ĭst) _____

18. (kĕm′ ĭ kəl) _____

B. Write these words in alphabetical order.

    chef   chocolate   chateau   chorus   chemist   chart

1. _____ 4. _____

2. _____ 5. _____

3. _____ 6. _____

Write the word that fits each definition.

1. _____ a lizard capable of changing color

2. _____ the founder of the Christian religion

3. _____ a chief cook

4. _____ an opportunity; a possibility

5. _____ a painful disease of the intestines

6. _____ a French castle

7. _____ a piece of iron fastened to a ship and dropped to the bottom of the water to hold the ship in place

8. _____ a yearly celebration of the birth of Christ

9. _____ a group of singers who sing together

10. _____ a person who studies chemicals

11. _____ a distinguishing feature or attribute

12. _____ a sheet of information arranged in diagrams

13. _____ very great confusion

14. _____ worthless stuff; rubbish

15. _____ pertaining to chemistry

16. _____ husked, roasted, and ground cacao seeds

17. _____ the qualities of fighting by a knight

18. _____ a person who makes plans for buildings

Write the spelling words three times.

1. chorus _____ _____

    _____

2. character _____ _____

    _____

3. anchor _____ _____

    _____

4. chaos _____ _____

    _____

5. chameleon _____ _____

    _____

6. chaff _____ _____

    _____

7. chance _____ _____

    _____

8. chemical _____ _____

    _____

9. chart _____ _____

    _____

10. chateau _____ _____

_____

11. chocolate _____ _____

_____

12. chef _____ _____

_____

13. chivalry _____ _____

_____

14. chemist _____ _____

_____

15. Christ _____ _____

_____

16. cholera _____ _____

_____

17. Christmas _____ _____

_____

18. architect _____ _____

_____

Unit 27

The spelling words in this unit are antonyms.

1. stretch
2. noisier
3. inward
4. shout
5. west
6. rounded
7. dull
8. difficult
9. arrive
10. shrink
11. quieter
12. outward
13. whisper
14. east
15. pointed
16. sharp
17. simple
18. leave

An **antonym** is a word that means the opposite, or nearly the opposite, of another word. For example, the antonym of **light** is **dark**.

Unit 27

1. stretch
2. noisier
3. inward
4. shout
5. west
6. rounded
7. dull
8. difficult
9. arrive
10. shrink
11. quieter
12. outward
13. whisper
14. east
15. pointed
16. sharp
17. simple
18. leave

A. Write the spelling word that is an **antonym** for each of these words.

1. dull _____ 2. east _____

3. stretch _____ 4. whisper _____

5. difficult _____ 6. arrive _____

B. Write the spelling words that are the comparative form of **quiet** and **noisy**.

1. _____ 2. _____

C. Write the spelling words that have the suffix **ward**.

1. _____ 2. _____

D. Write the spelling words that have the suffix **ed**.

1. _____ 2. _____

E. Write the three-syllable spelling words.

1. _____ 2. _____

3. _____

F. Write the two-syllable spelling words.

1. _____ 2. _____

3. _____ 4. _____

5. _____ 6. _____

7. _____

G. Write the spelling words that have the **long e** sound spelled with **ea**.

1. _____ 2. _____

A. Write these words in syllables. Put hyphens between the syllables.

1. noisier _____
2. inward _____
3. rounded _____
4. difficult _____
5. quieter _____
6. whisper _____
7. pointed _____
8. simple _____

B. Many years ago some English words were spoken and spelled differently than they are today. These pronunciations and spellings were called Middle English or Old English. Write the words you think came from these Middle English words.

1. shouten _____
2. shrinken _____
3. strecchen _____
4. whisperen _____

C. One word in each set is misspelled. Write the word correctly.

1. wesst, arrive, outward _____
2. stretch, simple, leeve _____
3. shrink, noisier, arive _____
4. quieter, eaest, shout _____

Complete the sentences with a spelling word that is an antonym of the underlined word.

1. Virginia is in the east, and California is in the _____.

2. A butter knife is dull, but a paring knife is _____.

3. We would _____ at church on time if we would leave earlier.

4. Playing an organ is simple, but learning to play a piano is more _____.

5. Your triceps will shrink while you _____ your biceps.

6. A revolving door will let some people walk inward while others are walking _____.

7. Some people shout loudly while others _____ quietly.

8. Some children talk noisier than others, and some talk _____ than others.

9. It is easier to write neatly with a pointed pencil than it is to write with a _____ one.

Write the spelling words three times.

1. stretch _____ _____

   _____

2. noisier _____ _____

   _____

3. inward _____ _____

   _____

4. shout _____ _____

   _____

5. west _____ _____

   _____

6. rounded _____ _____

   _____

7. dull _____ _____

   _____

8. difficult _____ _____

   _____

9. arrive _____ _____

   _____

10. shrink _____ _____

_____

11. quieter _____ _____

_____

12. outward _____ _____

_____

13. whisper _____ _____

_____

14. east _____ _____

_____

15. pointed _____ _____

_____

16. sharp _____ _____

_____

17. simple _____ _____

_____

18. leave _____ _____

_____

Unit 28

The spelling words in this unit are homophones.

1. wait
2. fair
3. sole
4. waste
5. bury
6. plain
7. sent
8. meat
9. break

10. weight
11. fare
12. soul
13. waist
14. berry
15. plane
16. scent
17. meet
18. brake

Homophones are words that sound alike but have different meanings and different spellings. Check to see how a word is used in a sentence to see which one to use.

Unit 28

1. wait
2. fair
3. sole
4. waste
5. bury
6. plain
7. sent
8. meat
9. break
10. weight
11. fare
12. soul
13. waist
14. berry
15. plane
16. scent
17. meet
18. brake

A. Write the spelling word that is a **homophone** for each of these words.

1. scent _____ 2. berry _____

3. wait _____ 4. soul _____

5. fair _____ 6. meat _____

7. waste _____ 8. plane _____

9. break _____

B. Write the spelling words that have the **long a** sound spelled by the letters **ai**.

1. _____ 2. _____

3. _____ 4. _____

C. Write the spelling word that has the **long a** sound spelled by the letters **ea**.

_____

D. Write the spelling words that have double letters.

1. _____ 2. _____

E. Write the spelling word that has the **long o** sound spelled by the letters **ou**.

_____

F. Write the spelling words that have the **long e** sound spelled by the letter **y**.

1. _____ 2. _____

G. Write the spelling word that has the **long o** sound spelled by the **o + consonant + e** spelling pattern.

_____

A. Write the two spelling words for each dictionary pronunciation.

1. (sōl) _____

2. (wāt) _____

3. (mēt) _____

4. (wāst) _____

5. (sĭnt) _____

6. (bĕr′ ē) _____

7. (fãr) _____

8. (plān) _____

9. (brāk) _____

B. Underline the spelling word in each sentence and write its part of speech.

1. Kevin and Patti did not get to board the plane. _____

2. The weather was fair on Saturday. _____

3. Please meet me at the mall. _____

4. My waist is too big. _____

5. I did not want to break the glass plate. _____

C. Write the word that matches each definition.

1. _____ the bottom of a shoe; the only person

2. _____ the inner person

3. _____ an odor

4. _____ the money to buy a ticket to travel

Fill in the blanks with the correct homonym.

1. If you want to slow down, push on the _____.

2. Greg was not the _____ owner of the business.

3. _____ apple seeds in the ground if you want an apple tree.

4. Don't _____ the glass plate.

5. We should prepare our _____ to spend eternity in Heaven.

6. The _____ of the skunk was very strong inside the school.

7. _____ me at church on Sunday morning.

8. Will you _____ for me to get there?

9. Do you want to eat just one _____?

10. You may ride a city bus if you pay the _____.

11. What kind of _____ do you want for dinner?

12. Did you hear about the _____ crash?

13. I _____ a book to John.

14. Two dollars was a _____ price for the swing.

15. We should never _____ money foolishly.

16. Order a _____ hamburger with nothing on it.

17. I have gained too much _____.

18. I am too big around the _____.

Write the spelling words three times.

1. wait _____ _____

   _____

2. fair _____ _____

   _____

3. sole _____ _____

   _____

4. waste _____ _____

   _____

5. bury _____ _____

   _____

6. plain _____ _____

   _____

7. sent _____ _____

   _____

8. meat _____ _____

   _____

9. break _____ _____

   _____

10. weight _____ _____

    _____

11. fare _____ _____

    _____

12. soul _____ _____

    _____

13. waist _____ _____

    _____

14. berry _____ _____

    _____

15. plane _____ _____

    _____

16. scent _____ _____

    _____

17. meet _____ _____

    _____

18. brake _____ _____

    _____

Unit 29

The spelling words in this unit show possession.

1. friend's
2. house's
3. group's
4. parent's
5. animal's
6. park's
7. brother's
8. town's
9. building's
10. friends'
11. houses'
12. groups'
13. parents'
14. animals'
15. parks'
16. brothers'
17. towns'
18. buildings'

The spelling words in this unit show two forms of possession. One form is the singular form. The other is the plural form. An apostrophe is used to show possession.

The possessive form of a singular noun is usually formed by adding **'s**. The possessive of a plural noun that ends in **s** is usually formed by adding an apostrophe after the **s**.

Unit 29

1. friend's
2. house's
3. group's
4. parent's
5. animal's
6. park's
7. brother's
8. town's
9. building's

10. friends'
11. houses'
12. groups'
13. parents'
14. animals'
15. parks'
16. brothers'
17. towns'
18. buildings'

A. Write the spelling words that are singular possessive forms.

1. _____ 2. _____

3. _____ 4. _____

5. _____ 6. _____

7. _____ 8. _____

9. _____

B. Write the spelling words that are plural possessive forms.

1. _____ 2. _____

3. _____ 4. _____

5. _____ 6. _____

7. _____ 8. _____

9. _____

C. Write the spelling words that begin with the consonant cluster **br**.

1. _____ 2. _____

D. Write the spelling words that begin with the consonant cluster **gr**.

1. _____ 2. _____

E. Write the spelling words that begin with the consonant cluster **fr**.

1. _____ 2. _____

F. Write the spelling words that have the letters **ing** in the last syllable.

1. _____ 2. _____

A. Write the spelling word that is a synonym for each word. Look closely to decide if it is the singular form or the plural form.

1. companion's _____

2. home's _____

3. city's _____

4. companions' _____

5. homes' _____

6. cities' _____

7. committee's _____

B. Write these spelling words in syllables. Put hyphens between the syllables.

1. parents' _____

2. animals' _____

3. brothers' _____

4. buildings' _____

C. Write these words in alphabetical order.

    group's   park's   friend's   parent's   building's   animal's

1. _____   4. _____

2. _____   5. _____

3. _____   6. _____

Fill in the blanks with spelling words.

1. An idea that came from one group is that _____ idea.

2. A room that belongs to two brothers is the _____ room.

3. If many buildings are under one roof, that roof is the _____ roof.

4. A suggestion that came from my friend is my _____ suggestion.

5. Mr. Abramson was our _____ mayor for many years.

6. The _____ designs on our street were of two different kinds.

7. My _____ house was new.

8. The _____ pool is not open in the winter.

9. The _____ cages at the zoo should be kept clean.

Write the spelling words three times.

1. friend's _____ _____

   _____

2. house's _____ _____

   _____

3. group's _____ _____

   _____

4. parent's _____ _____

   _____

5. animal's _____ _____

   _____

6. park's _____ _____

   _____

7. brother's _____ _____

   _____

8. town's _____ _____

   _____

9. building's _____ _____

   _____

10. friends' _____ _____

_____

11. houses' _____ _____

_____

12. groups' _____ _____

_____

13. parents' _____ _____

_____

14. animals' _____ _____

_____

15. parks' _____ _____

_____

16. brothers' _____ _____

_____

17. towns' _____ _____

_____

18. buildings' _____ _____

_____

Unit 30
Review

Ask your teacher for each test and record your grade after you have taken the test.

Part 1 Grade _____

Part 2 Grade _____

Part 3 Grade _____

Part 4 Grade _____

Unit 31

The spelling words in this unit are compound words.

1. drugstore
2. bluejay
3. barefoot
4. hairpin
5. password
6. goldfish
7. afternoon
8. chatterbox
9. pathway
10. underground
11. outboard
12. lifeboat
13. bedspread
14. downtown
15. outdoors
16. bricklayer
17. birdhouse
18. basketball

Two or more words can be put together to make a compound word. A compound word usually gets its meaning from the meanings of the two words.

Unit 31

1. drugstore
2. bluejay
3. barefoot
4. hairpin
5. password
6. goldfish
7. afternoon
8. chatterbox
9. pathway
10. underground
11. outboard
12. lifeboat
13. bedspread
14. downtown
15. outdoors
16. bricklayer
17. birdhouse
18. basketball

A. Finish the spelling words with the second word that makes up the compound word.

1. pass _____

2. under _____

3. after _____

4. down _____

5. drug _____

6. path _____

7. basket _____

8. bare _____

9. life _____

10. brick _____

11. hair _____

12. bed _____

13. blue _____

14. gold _____

15. chatter _____

16. bird _____

B. Write the two spelling words which contain the word **out**.

1. _____

2. _____

Write all the spelling words in alphabetical order.

1. _____
2. _____
3. _____
4. _____
5. _____
6. _____
7. _____
8. _____
9. _____
10. _____
11. _____
12. _____
13. _____
14. _____
15. _____
16. _____
17. _____
18. _____

Complete the sentences with spelling words. You will need to add **s** to two words.

1. Do not tell anyone your _____.

2. He went to the _____ to get his medicine.

3. We went to the court house which is _____.

4. I made a new _____ for our bed.

5. Kevin likes to watch a _____ game.

6. There was a _____ through the woods.

7. Isaiah made a _____ for his shop project.

8. Benjamin fed the _____ too much food.

9. Because Harold talked so much, he could have been considered a

   _____.

10. Some women wear _____ in their hair.

11. There were not enough _____ on the Titanic.

12. Students go home from school in the _____.

13. Take your shoes off and go _____.

14. You may go _____ to play if it is warm.

15. A _____ has a beautiful blue color.

16. Some animals make tunnels _____.

17. The _____ laid more bricks on the building.

18. You could find an _____ motor on a boat.

Write the spelling words two times each.

1. drugstore _____

   _____

2. bluejay _____

   _____

3. barefoot _____

   _____

4. hairpin _____

   _____

5. password _____

   _____

6. goldfish _____

   _____

7. afternoon _____

   _____

8. chatterbox _____

   _____

9. pathway _____

   _____

10. underground _____

    _____

11. outboard _____

_____

12. lifeboat _____

_____

13. bedspread _____

_____

14. downtown _____

_____

15. outdoors _____

_____

16. bricklayer _____

_____

17. birdhouse _____

_____

18. basketball _____

_____

Unit 32

These spelling words contain the letters **sc**.

1. scold
2. science
3. scorch
4. scene
5. scientific
6. describe
7. scarlet
8. scion
9. scenario
10. scapula
11. condescend
12. scenery
13. scooter
14. scoundrel
15. scribe
16. scarecrow
17. descent
18. scorpion

The **sc** can have the sound of **s** as in **scent**, or it can have the **sk** sound as in **score**.

Unit 32

1. scold
2. science
3. scorch
4. scene
5. scientific
6. describe
7. scarlet
8. scion
9. scenario
10. scapula
11. condescend
12. scenery
13. scooter
14. scoundrel
15. scribe
16. scarecrow
17. descent
18. scorpion

A. Write the spelling words that contain the **sc** and makes the **sk** sound.

1. _____ 2. _____

3. _____ 4. _____

5. _____ 6. _____

7. _____ 8. _____

9. _____ 10. _____

B. Write the spelling words that contain the **sc** and makes the **s** sound.

1. _____ 2. _____

3. _____ 4. _____

5. _____ 6. _____

7. _____ 8. _____

C. Write the spelling words that end with the letters **on**.

1. _____ 2. _____

D. Write the spelling word that has double vowels.

_____

E. Write the spelling words that have a **long i** sound.

1. _____ 2. _____

3. _____ 4. _____

5. _____

A. Write these words in syllables. Put hyphens between the syllables.

1. science _____
2. scientific _____
3. scorpion _____
4. scarlet _____
5. scion _____
6. scenario _____
7. scapula _____
8. scarecrow _____
9. scenery _____
10. condescend _____

B. One word in each set is misspelled. Write the word correctly

1. scene, scooter, skorch _____
2. scouter, scion, scientific _____
3. descent, scowdrel, scarlet _____
4. scarlet, scrib, scold _____
5. deskribe, scorpion, scold _____
6. condescend, scribe, desent _____
7. scorch, scean, scapula _____
8. skold, scientific, scion _____

Write the word that fits each definition.

1. _____ a mean or dishonorable person

2. _____ an area of knowledge that is an object of study

3. _____ a bright red color

4. _____ the act of going downward

5. _____ to burn slightly

6. _____ a grouping of things in a large view

7. _____ an animal, related to a spider but looks like a lobster

8. _____ to talk in written or spoken words

9. _____ an outline of a play

10. _____ to criticize, rebuke, reprimand

11. _____ the shoulder blade

12. _____ something used in science or the sciences

13. _____ a scholar and teacher of Jewish law

14. _____ to assume oneself has superiority

15. _____ the place where an event takes place

16. _____ a figure resembling a man used to frighten birds

17. _____ a shoot, bud, or twig grafted onto another plant

18. _____ a child's vehicle made of metal supported between two wheels

Write the spelling words three times.

1. scold _____ _____

   _____

2. science _____ _____

   _____

3. scorch _____ _____

   _____

4. scene _____ _____

   _____

5. scientific _____ _____

   _____

6. describe _____ _____

   _____

7. scarlet _____ _____

   _____

8. scion _____ _____

   _____

9. scenario _____ _____

   _____

10. scapula _____ _____
    _____

11. condescend _____
    _____
    _____

12. scenery _____ _____
    _____

13. scooter _____ _____
    _____

14. scoundrel _____ _____
    _____

15. scribe _____ _____
    _____

16. scarecrow _____ _____
    _____

17. descent _____ _____
    _____

18. scorpion _____ _____
    _____

Unit 33

These spelling words contain the letters **ear** with three different sounds.

1. yearn
2. weary
3. pear
4. dear
5. earnest
6. learn
7. fearless
8. gears
9. beard
10. earnings
11. wearing
12. early
13. hear
14. heard
15. nearby
16. appear
17. clear
18. yearling

The letters **ear** can have the **r-controlled** sound **er** as in **search**. They can have the **long e** sound as in **year**. They can also have the **air** sound as in **pear**. Use your spelling dictionary to find the pronunciation of a word if you are not sure of it.

Unit 33

1. yearn
2. weary
3. pear
4. dear
5. earnest
6. learn
7. fearless
8. gears
9. beard
10. earnings
11. wearing
12. early
13. hear
14. heard
15. nearby
16. appear
17. clear
18. yearling

A. Write the spelling words that contain the **r-controlled** sound as in **search**.

1. _____ 2. _____

3. _____ 4. _____

5. _____ 6. _____

B. Write the spelling words that contain the **long e** sound.

1. _____ 2. _____

3. _____ 4. _____

5. _____ 6. _____

7. _____ 8. _____

9. _____ 10. _____

C. Write the spelling words that contain the **r-controlled** sound as in **air**.

1. _____ 2. _____

D. Write the spelling words that contain the suffix **ing**.

1. _____ 2. _____

3. _____

E. Write the spelling words that have a **long e** sound spelled with a **y**.

1. _____ 2. _____

F. Write the spelling word that has a **long i** sound spelled with a **y**.

_____

A. Write the words for these dictionary pronunciations.

1. (yėrn) _____ 2. (pãr) _____

3. (dēr) _____ 4. (lėrn) _____

5. (gērs) _____ 6. (bērd) _____

7. (hēr) _____ 8. (klēr) _____

9. (hėrd) _____

B. Divide these words into syllables using hyphens. Use your spelling glossary.

1. weary _____

2. earnest _____

3. fearless _____

4. earnings _____

5. wearing _____

6. early _____

7. nearby _____

8. appear _____

9. yearling _____

C. Write the spelling word that fits the definition.

1. _____ showing sincerity of feeling

2. _____ to have a strong desire for

3. _____ money earned

Complete the sentences with spelling words.

1. If I walked five miles nonstop, I'd be _____.

2. Sometimes children _____ to go home from school.

3. The Fairdale library is _____ Angie's apartment.

4. Some small children seem to be _____ of heights.

5. My _____ were deposited into my account.

6. Mike had a big _____ on his face.

7. Will we leave _____ in the morning?

8. Have you _____ Denise sing?

9. An animal that is one year old is a _____.

10. Do you want an apple or a _____?

11. We should pray in _____ for soldiers.

12. Frankie's vision is not always _____.

13. Did James replace the _____ in the transmission?

14. Did you _____ what I said?

15. The greeting of many friendly letters begins with the word _____.

16. What was he _____ on his head to keep warm?

17. I want to _____ more about a computer.

18. Did Abigail _____ to be sick?

Write the spelling words three times.

1. yearn _____ _____

   _____

2. weary _____ _____

   _____

3. pear _____ _____

   _____

4. dear _____ _____

   _____

5. earnest _____ _____

   _____

6. learn _____ _____

   _____

7. fearless _____ _____

   _____

8. gears _____ _____

   _____

9. beard _____ _____

   _____

10. earnings _____ _____

_____

11. wearing _____ _____

_____

12. early _____ _____

_____

13. hear _____ _____

_____

14. heard _____ _____

_____

15. nearby _____ _____

_____

16. appear _____ _____

_____

17. clear _____ _____

_____

18. yearling _____ _____

_____

Unit 34

This unit has words that are plural words. Most of them have special spellings.

1. chiefs
2. cliffs
3. banjos
4. beliefs
5. cellos
6. reefs
7. roofs
8. heroes
9. radios
10. staffs
11. pianos
12. potatoes
13. tomatoes
14. piccolos
15. echoes
16. thieves
17. knives
18. tornadoes

To make words that end in **f** or **fe** plural, usually change the **f** or **fe** to **v** and add **es**. The exceptions to this rule are **chief**, **belief**, **reef**, and **roof**. Just add **s** to words ending in **ff**. To make the plural of words ending in **o**, add **s** to some. Add **es** to others. Check your glossary if you are not sure.

Unit 34

1. chiefs
2. cliffs
3. banjos
4. beliefs
5. cellos
6. reefs
7. roofs
8. heroes
9. radios
10. staffs
11. pianos
12. potatoes
13. tomatoes
14. piccolos
15. echoes
16. thieves
17. knives
18. tornadoes

A. Write the spelling words whose base words end in **f** or **fe** which do not follow the rule on page 204.

1. _____ 2. _____

3. _____ 4. _____

B. Write the spelling words whose base words end in **ff**.

1. _____ 2. _____

C. Write the spelling words whose base words end in **o** and to which **es** is added to form the plural.

1. _____ 2. _____

3. _____ 4. _____

5. _____

D. Write the spelling words whose base word ends in **o** and to which **s** is added to form the plural.

1. _____ 2. _____

3. _____ 4. _____

5. _____

E. Write the spelling words whose singular form ends in **f** or **fe** and who follow the rule on page 204 to make the plural form.

1. _____ 2. _____

F. Write the spelling words which have double consonants.

1. _____ 2. _____

3. _____ 4. _____

A. Write these words in syllables. Use hyphens between the syllables.

1. banjos _____ 2. beliefs _____

3. cellos _____ 4. heroes _____

5. radios _____ 6. pianos _____

7. potatoes _____

8. tomatoes _____

9. piccolos _____

10. echoes _____

11. tornadoes _____

B. Write the spelling word that is the plural form of these base words.

1. chief _____ 2. cliff _____

3. reef _____ 4. roof _____

5. staff _____ 6. thief _____

7. knife _____

C. Write these words in alphabetical order.

    potatoes   **echoes**   **radios**   **pianos**
    tornadoes   **heroes**   **tomatoes**   **piccolos**

1. _____ 5. _____

2. _____ 6. _____

3. _____ 7. _____

4. _____ 8. _____

A. Write spelling words that name musical instruments.

1. _____ 2. _____

3. _____ 4. _____

B. Write spelling words that name a kind of food.

1. _____ 2. _____

C. Write the spelling word that fits each definition.

1. _____ people who steal

2. _____ tops of buildings

3. _____ cutting utensils

4. _____ people who do brave deeds

5. _____ the main people of Indian tribes

6. _____ violent wind storms

7. _____ devices through which messages and music are transmitted by means of electricity and magnetic waves

8. _____ the high, steep fronts of hills overlooking a valley

9. _____ the repetition of a sound produced by reflection

10. _____ groups of people who work together

11. _____ ridges of rock just below the water's surface

12. _____ things believed, opinions

Write the spelling words three times.

1. chiefs _____ _____

   _____

2. cliffs _____ _____

   _____

3. banjos _____ _____

   _____

4. beliefs _____ _____

   _____

5. cellos _____ _____

   _____

6. reefs _____ _____

   _____

7. roofs _____ _____

   _____

8. heroes _____ _____

   _____

9. radios _____ _____

   _____

10. staffs _____ _____

_____

11. pianos _____ _____

_____

12. potatoes _____ _____

_____

13. tomatoes _____ _____

_____

14. piccolos _____ _____

_____

15. echoes _____ _____

_____

16. thieves _____ _____

_____

17. knives _____ _____

_____

18. tornadoes _____ _____

_____

Unit 35

These spelling words are the same in their singular and plural form.

1. moose
2. honey
3. spinach
4. sheep
5. broccoli
6. spaghetti
7. bacon
8. deer
9. popcorn
10. wheat
11. cattle
12. butter
13. oatmeal
14. trout
15. zucchini
16. bread
17. shrimp
18. haddock

Unit 35

1. moose
2. honey
3. spinach
4. sheep
5. broccoli
6. spaghetti
7. bacon
8. deer
9. popcorn
10. wheat
11. cattle
12. butter
13. oatmeal
14. trout
15. zucchini
16. bread
17. shrimp
18. haddock

A. Write the spelling words that have double vowels..

1. _____   2. _____

3. _____

B. Write the spelling words that have double consonants.

1. _____   2. _____

3. _____   4. _____

5. _____   6. _____

C. Write the spelling words that are compound words.

1. _____   2. _____

D. Write the spelling word that ends with a consonant digraph.

_____

E. Write the spelling words that begin with a consonant digraph.

1. _____   2. _____

3. _____

F. Vowels are missing from these words. Fill in the missing vowels.

1. b ____ c ____ n   2. wh ____ ____ t

3. tr ____ ____ t   4. br ____ ____ d

5. shr ____ mp   6. h ____ n ____ y

7. br ____ cc ____ l ____   8. sp ____ gh ____ tt ____

A. Write the one-syllable spelling words.

1. _____ 2. _____

3. _____ 4. _____

5. _____ 6. _____

7. _____

B. Write the two-syllable spelling words.

1. _____ 2. _____

3. _____ 4. _____

5. _____ 6. _____

7. _____ 8. _____

C. Write the three-syllable spelling words.

1. _____ 2. _____

3. _____

D. Write the spelling word that fits each definition.

1. _____ a fish smaller than the cod

2. _____ a summer squash of bushy growth with smooth cylindrical dark green fruits

3. _____ a plant having large green leaves eaten as a vegetable

4. _____ long-tailed shell fish that live in the ocean

A. Write the spelling words that name an animal or something that comes from an animal.

1. _____ 2. _____

3. _____ 4. _____

5. _____ 6. _____

7. _____ 8. _____

9. _____ 10. _____

B. Write the spelling word that names a plant or something that comes from a plant.

1. _____ 2. _____

3. _____ 4. _____

5. _____ 6. _____

7. _____ 8. _____

C. Write two sentences telling about your favorite food.

_____

_____

_____

_____

Write the spelling words three times.

1. moose _____ _____

   _____

2. honey _____ _____

   _____

3. spinach _____ _____

   _____

4. sheep _____ _____

   _____

5. broccoli _____ _____

   _____

6. spaghetti _____ _____

   _____

7. bacon _____ _____

   _____

8. deer _____ _____

   _____

9. popcorn _____ _____

   _____

10. wheat _____ _____

_____

11. cattle _____ _____

_____

12. butter _____ _____

_____

13. oatmeal _____ _____

_____

14. trout _____ _____

_____

15. zucchini _____ _____

_____

16. bread _____ _____

_____

17. shrimp _____ _____

_____

18. haddock _____ _____

_____

Unit 36
Review

Ask your teacher for each test and record your grade after you have taken the test.

Part 1 Grade _____

Part 2 Grade _____

Part 3 Grade _____

Part 4 Grade _____

Spelling Glossary Pronunciations

ă cat map

ā age, race

ä father, calm

ã care, air

ĕ red, bed

ē eat, he

ė mother, heard

ĭ is, it

ī ice, ride

ŏ hot, cot

ō over, go

ô ball, caught

oi oil, boy

ou house, out

ŭ up, cup

ū use, few

ü rule, move

ů pure, sure

ə represents.
a in about
e in taken
i in pencil
o in lemon
u in circus

absentee

Aa

ab-sen-tee (ăb·sĭn·tē′) n. someone not present:

ac-cep-tance (ăk sĕp′ təns)
ac·cep·tance n.
1. agreement to an invitation or offer: a written or verbal indication that somebody agrees to an invitation or offer
2. act of willingly taking a gift: the willing receipt of a gift or payment

ache (āk) n. constant pain: a feeling of constant dull pain 2. v. to be in pain. [Old English æce (noun), acan (verb), origin]

ac-tor (ăk′ tər) n. performer in plays: somebody who acts in plays, movies, or television [From Middle English, from Latin *actor*, a doer]

a-do-be (ə dō′ bē) 1. n. earthen brick: brick made from earth and straw and dried by the sun 2. building made of adobe: a structure made with adobe bricks

a-dopt (ə dŏpt′) v. to approve officially

ad-ven-ture (ăd vĭn′ chər) n. an exciting happening [From Latin *adventuras*, adventure from *asvenire*, to arrive]

a-far (ə fär′) adv. far away

appointment

af-ter-noon (ăf′ tər nün′) n. the part of the day after noon and before evening

air-line (ãr līn′) n. an airplane company

a-larm (ə lärm′) n. a signal that gives a warning of a fire or some other danger

a-lert (ə lėrt′) 1. n. a warning or alarm 2. v. to warn or alarm

al-li-ga-tor (ăl′ ə gā′ tər) n. a large water animal with a long, thick tail

an-chor (ăng′ kər) n. a weight that,when thrown overboard, keeps a boat from moving

an-cient (ān′ shənt) adj. very old [From Latin *antineanus*, going before, from Latin, *ante*, before]

an-i-mal (ăn′ ə məl) n. a living, moving creature that is not a plant
possessive belonging to one - **animal's**
possessive belonging to more than one - **animals'**

a-part-ment (ə pärt′ mənt) n. one or more rooms used to live in

ap-pear (ə pēr′) v. to come into view, or become visible

ap-point-ment (ə point′ mənt) n. a special time set aside for a meeting

a-quar-i-um (ə kwâr′ ē əm) *n.* a tank in which fish are kept and exhibited

ar-chi-tect (är′ kĭ tĕkt′) *n.* a person whose profession is to design large constuctions or buildings

ar-gue (är′ gū) *v.* to present reasons for or against a thing

ar-range (ə rānj′) *v.* to put things in a special order

ar-rive (ə rīv′) *v.* to get to a certain place

a-round (ə round′) *adv.* in a circle or ring

ar-row (ăr′ ō) *n.* 1. a pointed stick that is shot from a bow 2. *n.* a pointed symbol that shows direction

as-sis-tant (ə sĭs′ tənt) *n.* a person who gives aid, a helper

at-tach (ə tăch′) *v.* to fasten or join; connect

auc-tion-eer (ôk′ shə nēr) *n.* a person who conducts sales at an auction

Au-gust (ô′ gəst) *n.* the eighth month of the year

au-thor (ô′ thər) *n.* a person who writes books or stories

au-to-mat-ic (ô′ tə măt′ ĭk) *adj.* able to work by itself

au-to-mo-bile (ô′ tə mō bĭl) *n.* a car

au-tumn (ô′ təm) *n.* the fall season of the year between summer and winter

av-e-nue (ăv′ ə nū) *n.* a street [From Old French *avenir,* to approach, from Latin *advenire,* to come to]

aw-ful (ô′ fəl) *adj.* terrible; horrible

B b

back-ward (băk′ wərd) *adv.* Also **back-wards.** 1. toward the back or rear 2. toward the past or starting point 3. with the back first

ba-con (bā′ kən) *n.* meat from the back and sides of a hog, usually salted or smoked

bak-er (bā′ kər) *n.* a person who bakes and sells breads and cakes

ban-jo (băn′ jō) *n. pl.* **ban-jos** a musical instrument having strings stretched over a shallow frame covered with skin. It is plucked with the fingers or a pick.

bare-foot (bâr′ foot′) *adv.* without shoes

bar-rel (bãr′ əl) *n.* a container with sides that curve out slightly

basketball

bas-ket-ball (băs′ kĭt bôl′) *n.* 1. a game played by two five-man teams on a court having a raised basket at each end 2. the ball used in this game

beard (bērd) *n* the hair on a man's chin and, often, his neck and cheeks.

beau-ti-ful (bū′ tə fəl) *adj.* very pretty

be-cause (bĭ kôz′) *conj.* for the reason that.

bed-spread (bĕd′ sprĕd) *n.* an outer covering for a bed

be-have (bĭ hāv′) *v.* to act correctly

be-lief (bĭ lēf′) *n.* pl. **be-liefs**
1. something believed; opinion.
2. religious faith

be-lieve (bĭ lēv′) *v.* to think somthing is real or true

bench (bĭnch) *n. pl.* **benches** a long seat, usually made of wood. [From Old English *benc,* bench]

be-neath ((bĭ nēth′) *prep.* under

ber-ry (bĕr′ ē) *n. pl.* **ber-ries** a small juicy fruit.

bridle

bi-cy-cle (bī′ sĭk′ əl)) 1. *n.* a two-wheeled object to ride. 2. *adj.* having to do with a bicycle Ex. Please stay on the bicycle path.

bird-house (bėrd′ hous) *n.* a place for birds to live

birth (bėrth) *n.* the act of being born

blew (blü) *v.* the past tense of blow

blue-jay (blü′ jā) *n.* a bird with blue feathers

bor-der (bōr′ dėr) *n.* the edge of something that forms its outer boundary

bore (bōr) *n.* something that's not of interest

bought (bôt) *v.* the past tense of buy

brake (brāk) *n.* a device for slowing or stopping a vehicle that is in motion.

break (brāk) *v.* 1. to interrupt 2. to crack something

bread (brĕd) *n.* food made of baked dough or batter.

brick-lay-er (brĭk′ lā′ ėr) *n.* a person who builds with bricks.

bri-dle (brī′ dəl) *n.* the part of a harness that slips over a horse's head.

broccoli

broc-co-li (brŏk′ ə lē) *n.* a kind of cauliflower with green stalks and flowerlike heads used as a vegetable.

bro-chure (brō shůr′) *n.* a booklet or pamphlet

broth-er (brŭth′ ər) *n.* a boy or man who has the same mother or father as another person. *possessive belonging to one -* **brother's** *possessive belonging to more than one –***brothers'**

brought (brôt) *v.* did bring

budg-et (bŭj′ ĭt) *n.* a plan for spending that includes money received and spent.

build-ing (bĭl′ dĭng) *n.* a structure such as a house or store. *possessive form of building,* **building's** *possessive plural form of building* **buildings'**

bur-y (bĕr′ ē) *v.* to put in the ground

bus-y (bĭz′ ē) *adj.* having plenty to do **busiest** superlative form of busy

but-ter (bŭt′ ər) *n.* the fatty portion of milk, which separates as a soft whitish or yellowish solid when milk is churned

celebrate

C c

cac-tus (kăk′ tŭs) *n. pl.* **cactuses** or **cacti**
a plant having a fleshy stem and spines instead of leaves; native to the hot, dry regions of America

caf-e-ter-i-a (kăf′ ə tēr′ ē ə) *n.* a restaurant where people pick up their own food

ca-noe (kə nü′) 1. *n.* a small boat with pointed ends that is moved with one paddle

cap-i-tal (kăp′ ə təl) *n.* the location of the government

cap-ture (kăp′ chər) *v.* to take by force or skill

care-less (kãr′ lĭs) *adj.* not being careful about what one does

car-go (kär′ gō) *n.* goods that are carried by ship

cat-tle (kăt′ əl) *n.* animals of the ox family, such as cows and bulls

cause (kôz) *n.* what makes something happen

ceil-ing (sē′ lĭng) *n.* the overhead interior lining of a room

cel-e-brate (sĕl′ ə brāt) *v.* to have a party for a special occasion

cello

cel-lo (chĕl′ ō) *n. pl.* **cel-los** a large instrument of the violin family between a viola and a double bass in size and range. It is held between the knees when played.

cer-tain-ly (sėrt′ ən lē) *adv.* without a doubt

chaff (chăf) *n.* 1. the husks of grains and grasses that are usually separated while threshing. 2. worthless matter; rubbish [from the Old English word *ceaf*]

cha-grin (shə grĭn′) *n.* annoyance caused by failure or disappoinment

chaise (shāz) a light, open carriage with a hood

cham-ber (chām′ bər) *n. 1.* a room in a house or apartment 2. a judge's consultation room [from Old French *chambre*]

cha-me-le-on (kə mēl′ yən) *n.* a kind of a lizard that can change the color of its skin to match its surroundings

cham-pi-on (chăm′ pē ən) *n.* the winner of a contest. [From Old French *champion*, champion, from Latin *campus,* field]

chance (chăns) *n.* 1. the unpredictable way in which things happen 2. a possibility of anything happening

check

chan-de-lier (shăn′ də lēr′) *n.* a light fixture, usually elaborate in design, that is suspended from a ceiling

change (chānj) *v.* to make or become different

chan-nel (chăn′ əl) *n.* a path cut by water

cha-os (kā′ ŏs) *n.* a state of utter confusuion

char-ac-ter (kăr′ ĭk tər) *n.* the total of traits and qualities that make up the individual nature of a person or thing

char-i-ty (chăr′ ĭ tē) *n.* the act of goodwill toward humanity; love

chart (chärt) *n.* 1. a map 2. a sheet showing information in the form of a graph

cha-teau (shă tō′) *n.* a castle in France

chat-ter-box (chăt′ ər bŏks) *n.* a person who talks or chatters a lot

chauf-feur (shō′ fər) *n.* 1. a person employed to drive another's automobile 2. *v.* to drive or work as a chauffeur

check (chĕk) *n.* a mark placed beside an item

cheering

cheer-ing (chēr′ ĭng) *v.* the act of shouting approval for someone or a team

cheese (chēz) *n.* a solid food made from sour milk

chef (shĕf) *n.* a chief cook, usually a man, in charge of other cooks

chem-i-cal (kĭm′ ĭ kəl) *n.* a substance used in chemistry

chem-ist (kĭm′ ĭst) *n.* a person who is skilled in chemistry

Chi-ca-go (shĭ kä′ gō) *n.* a city in Northeast Illinois, second largest city in the United States

chief (chēf) *n. pl.* **chiefs** the leader of a group

chis-el (chĭz′ əl) *n.*1. a sharp tool used to cut wood, stone, or metal 2. *v.* to cut or shape with a chisel

chiv-al-ry (shĭv′ əl rē) *n.* the qualities that were expected of knights which included bravery, courtesy, and loyalty

choc-o-late (chô′ kə lĭt) *n.* food or flavoring, typically a smooth sweet brown solid, made from roasted and ground cacao seeds usually sweetened and mixed with cocoa butter and dried milk

city

chol-er-a (kŏl′ ə rə) *n.* an acute, often fatal, infectious disease of the intestines that causes diarrhea, cramps, and vomiting

choose (chüz) *v.* to select [From Old English *chosen*, from Old English *ceosan*, to choose]

chop-per (chŏp′ ər) *n.* something that chops

chore (chôr) *n. pl.* **chores** a small job performed at fixed times.

cho-rus (kôr ′ əs) *n.* a group of singers

cho-sen (chō′ zən) *v.* the past participle of choose

Christ (krīst) *n.* a name for Jesus, the founder of the Christian religion

Christ-mas (krĭst′ məs) *n.* the yearly celebration of the birth of Jesus

church (chėrch) *n.* a building used for public worship

chute (shüt) *n.* a sloping shaft, for moving things downward

cir-cu-lar (sėr′ kū lər) *adj.* in the shape of a circle; round

cit-y (sĭt′ ē) *n. pl.* **cities** a very large town

clear

clear (klēr) *adj.* free from darkness; bright

clerk (klėrk) *n.* a salesperson

cliff (klĭf) *n. pl.* **cliffs** a high, steep front of a rocky mass or hill overlooking a lower area

clue (klü) *n.* a hint that helps solve a mystery

coach (kōch) *n.* 1. a large, horse-drawn, four-wheeled carriage 2. a person who trains or instructs athletes

co-au-thor (kō ô′ thər) *n.* someone who helps another write a book or story

co-di-rec-tor (kō dĭ rĕk′ tər) *n.* a person who helps another direct, manage, or supervise a play or movie

col-lect-or (kə lĕkt′ ėr) *n.* a person who gathers things of the same kind

col-o-ny (kŏl′ ə nē) *n.* a group of people, plants, or animals that settle somewhere together

com-bine (kəm bīn′) *v.* to bring or join together; unite; mix

com -mu-ni-ty (kə mū′ nə tē) *n.* a group of people living in the same area

conspire

com-pa-ny (kŭm′ pə nē) *n.* a group of people joined together for the purpose of business

com-pare (kŭm pãr′) *v.* to determine how two or more things are similar or different

com-pel (kŭm pĕl′) *v.* to force or drive

com-pile (kŭm pīl′) *v.* to put or gather in one list, book, etc.

com-plain (kŭm plān′) *v.* to talk about one's pains or problems

com-plete (kŭm plēt′) *v.* 1. to finish 2. *adj.* finished

con-ceal (kŭn sēl′) *v.* to hide from sight

con-crete (kŏn′ krēt) 1. *n.* cement 2. *adj.* made of cement

con-de-scend (kŏn′ dĭ sĭnd′) *v.* to assume oneself has superiority

con-duct (kŏn′ dŭkt) *n.* a way of behaving or acting

con-fi-dence (kŏn′ fĭ dəns) *n.* 1. full trust or belief in a person or thing 2. trust in oneself 3. in secret or as a secret; privately

con-spire (kŭn spīr′) *v.* to act or work together toward the same goal

con-sume (kŭn süm′) *v.* to use up or spend

con-tin-u-ous (kŭn tĭn′ ū əs) *adj.* without stopping

co-op-er-ate (kō ŏp′ ə rāt′) *v.* to work together willingly with someone for a common purpose

cor-ner (kōr′ nėr) *n.* a place where two sides meet

cough (kôf) *n.* a sudden forcing of air through the throat

cou-ple (kŭp′ əl) *n.* a pair; two things or persons who go together

cou-ra-geous (kə rā′ jəs) *adj.* having courage

cous-in (kŭz′ ən) *n.* the child of one's uncle or aunt

crane (krān) *n.* a machine for lifting heavy objects

cre-a-tive (krē ā′ tĭv) *adj.* having the ability to create

crew (krü) *n.* a group of people working together

crum-ble (krŭm′ bəl) *v.* to break into small pieces

cuff (kŭf) *n. pl.* **cuffs** the band of material at the bottom of a sleeve or the turned up fold at the bottom of pant legs

cur-ly (kėr′ lē) *adj.* wavy or in twists

curve (kėrv) *n.* a bend; a line that is not straight

cus-tom-er (kŭs′ tə mər) *n.* a shopper; a person one has to deal with

cy-clone (sī ′ klōn) *n.* a weather system in which an area of low barometric pressure is surrounded by a circular flow of wind

D d

daily (dā′ lē) *adv.* every day

dan-ger-ous (dān′ jə rəs) *adj.* not safe

dear (dēr) *adj.* beloved or loved; favorite

deer (dēr) *n. pl.* **deer** any of numerous swift-running, hoofed, cud-chewing animals

de-pend-a-ble (dĭ pĭn′ də bəl) *adj.* worthy of trust; reliable

de-pend-ence (dĭ pĭn′ dəns) *n.* the state of depending on or needing someone or something

descent

de-scent (dĭ sĭnt') *n.* the act of going down a downward slope

de-scribe (dĭ skrīb') *v.* to tell in written or spoken words

de-ter-gent (dĭ tėr' jənt) *n.* a cleaning agent

dif-fi-cult (dĭf' ə kŭlt) *adj.* hard to do

dis-a-gree (dĭs' ə grē') *v.* to differ; to argue

dis-ap-prove (dĭs' ə prüv') *v.* to consider that something is not right

dis-com-fort (dĭs kŭm' fərt) *n.* uneasiness

dis-cour-te-sy (dĭs kėr' tə sē) *n.* impoliteness

dis-ease (də zēz') *n.* a sickness

dis-hon-or (dĭs ŏn' ėr) *v.* to bring disgrace to

dis-please (dĭs plēz') *v.* to make unhappy

dis-tance (dĭs' təns) *n.* the space between two things

di-vide (də vīd') *v.* to separate or cut into pieces

elementary

down-town (doun' toun) *adv.* in the main section or business center of a town

drug-store (drŭg' stōr) *n.* a store where medicines are sold

dull (dŭl) *adj.* 1. boring 2. not sharp

dump (dŭmp) *n.* 1. *n.* a place for trash 2. *v.* to unload in a pile or get rid of something

du-ty (dü' tē) *n.* a responsibility or job

E e

ear-ly (ėr' lē) *adv.* in or during the first part of a period of time

ear-nest (ėr' nĭst) *adj.* serious in intention, purpose, or effort

earn-ings (ėr' nĭngz) *n.* money earned; wages or profits

east (ēst) *n.* the direction from which the sun rises

ech-o (ĕk' ō) *n. pl.* **ech-oes** to repeat a sound

eight (āt) *n.*, *adj.* one more than seven *adj.* Ex. He had eight dollars.

el-e-men-ta-ry (ĕl' ə mĕn' tə rē) *adj.* referring to or dealing with elements or basic principles

employee

em-ploy-ee (ĕm ploi′ ē) *n.* a person working for another person or a business

en-gi-neer (ĕn′ jə nēr′) *n.* a person who is trained in one of the branches of engineering

en-large (ĕn lärj′) *v.* to make or become bigger

en-rich (ĕn rĭch′) *v.* to supply with riches; to supply with something desirable

en-tan-gle (ĕn tăng′ gəl) *v.* 1. to catch in a tangle 2. to involve in anything like a tangle

e-rase (ĭ rās′) *v.* to rub out of sight or wipe off

ex-cel-lent (ĕks′ sə lənt) *adj.* very good

ex-change (ĕks chānj′) *v.* to give up something and get something else in its place

ex-cuse (ĕk skyūz′) *v.* to pardon or forgive; overlook
excused excusing

ex-er-cise′ (ĕk′ sėr sīz) *n.* an activity that involves moving the body

ex-plore (ĕk splōr′) *v.* to study an area carefully with the intent to discover something

finish

ex-port (ĕks pōrt′) *v.* to send goods to another country for sale

F f

fa-cial (fā′ shəl) *adj.* 1. of or located on the face 2. used on the face

fair (făr) 1. *n.* a show of farm goods and home-made items 2. *adj.* with clear, pleasant weather

faith (fāth) *n.* 1. trust or confidence in a person or thing 2. belief that is not based on proof 3. a belief in God

fare (făr) *n.* the money you pay to buy a ticket to travel on a bus, train, or plane

far-ther (făr′ thər) *adv.* a greater distance

fear-less (fēr′ lĭs) *adj.* without fear; brave

feast (fēst) *n.* a special meal

fes-ti-val (fĕs′ tə vəl) *n.* a celebration or party

fe-ver (fē′ vėr) *n.* an abnormally high body temperature

fi-nal-ly (fī′ nəl ē) *adv.* after a long time

fin-ish (fĭn′ ĭsh) *v.* to complete; to reach the end.

flannel

flan-nel (flăn′ əl) *n.* a warm, soft, napped cloth usually made of cotton or wool

flare (flãr) *v.* 1. to blaze with a sudden burst of flame *n.* 2. a blaze of fire or light used for a signal

flirt (flėrt) *v.* to play at courting

fo-cus (fō′ kəs) *n.* 1. the central point of attraction *v.* 2. to concentrate at a single point of attraction

fool-ish (fü′ lĭsh) *adj.* not wise

for-bid (fōr bĭd′) *v.* not to allow

force (fōrs) *n.* 1. a strong power *v.* 2. to drive or propel with strength.

for-ty (fōr′ tē) *n.* 1. a number that is four times ten. *adj.* amounting to forty in number Ex. *forty people*

fought (fôt) *v.* did fight

frac-tion (frăk′ shən) *n.* one or more parts of a whole.

freight (frāt) *n.* a train for carrying goods instead of passengers.

friend (frĭnd) *n.* a companion which you like very much **friend's**, *possessive for one friend;* **friends'** *possessive for more than one friend*

gorilla

fruit (früt) *n.* the edible part of a plant that develops from the flower and encloses the seed.

fu-ture (fū′ chėr) *n.* the time yet to come

Gg

ga-ze-bo (gə zē′ bō) *n. pl.* **gazebos** *or* **gazeboes** a small building with view: a small, usually open-sided and slightly elevated building, situated in a spot for people to have a pleasant view

gears (gērz) *n.* wheels with toothed edges that work together to provide a particular direction or speed of rotation

ge-om-e-try *n.* (jē ŏm′ ĭ trē) *n.* the branch of math that deals with points, lines, angles, surfaces, and solids, and the properties and measurement of area space

glove (glŭv) *n.* a covering for the hand which has separate places for the fingers

gold-en (gōl′ dən) *adj.* having a bright yellow color

gold-fish (gōld′ fĭsh) *n.* a small orange or yellow fish sometimes kept as a pet

go-ril-la (gə rĭl′ ə) *n.* the largest member of the ape family

government

gov-ern-ment (gŭv′ ėrn mĭnt) *n.* people who rule a country; a system of rule for a country, state, or area

grain (grān) *n.* a cereal plant such as oats, wheat, and corn

gram-mar (grăm′ ėr) *n.* the study of word forms and their uses in sentences

grease (grēs) *n.* a thick, oily liquid

gro-cer-y (grō′ sər ē) *n.* a store that sells food

group (grüp) *n.* a collection
group's *possessive for one group*
groups' *possessive for more than one group*

grove (grōv) *n.* a small group of trees

growth (grōth) *n.* an increase

guess (gĕs) *v.* to judge or arrive at an answer without having all the facts

gym-na-si-um (jĭm nā′ zē əm) *n.* a building or room designed and equipped for athletic activities

H h

had-dock *n. pl.* **haddock** a fish of the North Atlantic, smaller than the cod

hair-pin (hãr′ pĭn) *n.* a small clip used to hold hair in place

house

har-bor (här′ bėr) *n.* a sheltered area where ships can dock

hard-en (härd′ ən) *v.* to make more firm

har-ness (här′ nĭs) *n.* a piece of leather used to hitch a horse to an object

haul (hôl) *v.* to drag or carry heavy objects.

hear (hēr) *v.* to receive sounds through the ear

heard (hėrd) *v.* past tense of hear

he-ro (hē′ rō) *n. pl.* **he-roes** a person who is admired for his courage and a noble deed

hol-low (hŏl′ ō) *adj.* having nothing but air inside of a thing

hon-ey (hŭn′ ē) *n.* a sweet substance produced by bees and stored in their hives for food

hos-pi-tal (hŏs′ pĭ təl) *n.* an institution where sick or injured people are given medical care

house (hous) *n.* a building in which people live **house's** *possessive for one house*
houses' *possessive for more than one house*

hu-man (hyū′ mən) *n.* of, referring to, or characteristic of mankind

I i

im-por-tance (ĭm pōr′ təns) *n.* the quality of being important

im-pos-si-ble ((ĭm pŏs′ ə bəl) *adj.* not possible; unable to exist or happen

im-pres-sive (ĭm prĕs′ ĭv) *adj.* making a strong impression on the mind

im-pure (ĭm pyūr′) *adj.* not pure; dirty

in-ac-tive (ĭn ăk′ tĭv) *adj.* not active; sluggish

in-ca-pa-ble (ĭn kā′ pə bəl) *adj.* not capable; not having the ability or power to do something

in-deed (ĭn dēd′) 1. *adv.* certainly; really
2. *inter.* an expression of surprise

in-jure (ĭn′ jėr) *v.* to hurt; to harm

in-tro-duce (ĭn trə düs′) *v.* to become or make acquainted with someone or something

in-ward (ĭn′ wėrd) *adv.* toward the center

ir-reg-u-lar (ĭ rĕg′ ū lėr) *adj.* not evenly shaped or formed

ir -re- place-a-ble (ĭ rĭ plā′ sə bəl) *adj.* incapable of being replaced

J j

jour-ney (jėr′ nē) *n.* a long trip

judge (jŭj) *v.* to make a decision about a situation after examining the facts. **judging**

jum-ble (jŭm′ bəl) *n.* a mixed-up mess

jum-bo (jŭm′ bō) *adj.* large

June (jün) *n.* the sixth month of the year

K k

knife (nīf) *n. pl.* **knives** a tool, used for cutting, having a sharp-edged metal blade set into a handle.

L l

la-bel (lā′ bəl) *n.* a tag that gives information about the thing to which it is attached.

laun-dry (lŏn′ drē) *n.* 1. a place where clothes are washed. 2. clothes that are to be washed.

learn (lėrn) *v.* to acquire knowledge or skill

leave (lēv) *v.* to go [From Middle English *leven*, leave]

legal

le-gal (lē′ gəl) *adj.* lawful; having to do with the law

le-gal-i-ty (lē goul′ ĭ tē) *n.* the state of being lawful

life-boat (līf bōt′) *n.* a small life-saving boat

light-ning (līt′ nĭng) *n.* a sudden flash of light in clouds

lo-cate (lō′ kāt) *v.* to find something

loose (lüs) *adj.* not tight, not attached tightly

lose (lüz) *v.* to misplace; to have something no longer

lo-tion (lō′ shən) *n.* a liquid applied to the skin.

M m

mag-a-zine (măg′ ə zēn) *n.* a publication printed periodically.

ma-jor (mā′ jėr) 1. *n.* a military officer 2. *adj.* more important

mal-nour-ished (măl nėr′ ĭshd′) *adj.* poorly nourished

mal-treat (măl trēt′) *v.* to treat badly

mar-vel-ous (mär′ və ləs) *adj.* amazing

misunderstand

meas-ure (mĕzh′ ėr) *v.* to find the size of an object

meat (mēt) *n.* the flesh of animals used for food

meet (mēt) *v.* to be introduced to a person for the first time

mid-night (mĭd′ nīt) *n.* the middle of the night or at 12:00 o'clock A.M.

mid-stream (mĭd strēm′) *n.* the middle of a stream

mid-week (mĭd wēk′) *n* in the middle of the week

mil-lion-aire (mĭl′ yə nãr′) *n.* a very rich person

mis-be-have (mĭs bĭ hāv′) *v.* to act badly

mis-di-rect (mĭs də rĕkt′) *v.* to give someone the wrong directions

mis-er-a-ble (mĭz′ ėr ə bəl) *adj.* very unhappy; of wretched character or quality

mis-spell (mĭs spĕl′) *v.* to spell a word incorrectly

mis-un-der-stand (mĭs′ ŭn dėr stănd′) *v.* to get the wrong meaning

moose

moose (müs) *n. pl.* **moose** a very large animal of the deer family found in the United States and Canada

mo-tor-cy-cle (mō′ tėr sī′ kəl) *n.* a two-wheeled vehicle, similar to a bike, driven with a gasoline engine

mul-ti-ply (mŭl′ tə plī) *v.* to increase a number a given number of times

N n

nat-ur-al (năch′ ėr əl) *adj.* produced or supplied by nature

na-ture (nā′ chėr) *n.* the outdoor world

near-by (nēr′ bī) *adj. adv.* close at hand; not far off

nec-es-sar-y (něs′ ə sãr′ ē) *adj.* needed

neigh-bor (nā′ bėr) *n.* a person who lives next door or nearby

nei-ther (nē′ thėr or nī′ thėr) *conj.* not either; nor; no more

nerve (nėrv) *n.* a fiber through which physical feelings are carried

nick-el (nĭk′ əl) *n.* 1. a hard, silvery metal used in alloys and for plating metals 2. a coin worth five cents

nine-teen (nīn tēn′) *n. adj.* one more than eighteen; *adj. Ex.* He was eighteen years old.

orchard

nine-ty (nīn tē′) *n. adj.* ten times nine *adj. Ex.* The tires cost ninety dollars.

nois-y (noi′ zē) *adj.* loud **nois-i-er**

none (nŭn) *pron.* not any

non-liv-ing (nŏn lĭv′ ĭng) *adj.* not alive

non-res-i-dent (nŏn rĕz′ ə dĭnt) *n.* one who does not live in a certain area

non-sense (nŏn′ sĭns) *n.* foolishness

non-stop (nŏn′ stŏp) *adv.* without stopping

nor-mal (nōr′ məl) *adj.* regular; natural; of the standard kind.

north-ern (nōr′ thėrn) *adj.* of or referring to the north

nov-el-ist (nŏv′ ə lĭst) *n.* a person who writes novels

O o

oat-meal (ōt′ mēl) *n.* meal made from oats

o-bey (ō bā′) *v.* to do as one is ordered

o-cean (ō′ shən) *n.* a large body of salt water

or-bit (ōr′ bĭt) *v.* to go around a planet

or-chard (ōr′ chėrd) *n.* the place where fruit trees are grown

or-di-nar-y (ōrd′ ən ãr′ ē) *adj.* the usual

ought (ôt) *v.* should

out-board (out′ bōrd) *adj.* outside a boat

out-doors (out′ dōrz) *adv.* out of doors; in the open air

out- ward (out′ wėrd) *adv.* away from the center

P p

par-don (pärd′ ən) *v.* to excuse; to forgive

par-ent (pãr′ ənt) *n.* a father or mother **parent's**, *possessive for one parent;* **parents'** *possessive for more than one parent*

park (pärk) *n.* a public place for recreation **park's**; *possessive for one park;* **parks'** *possessive for more than one park*

pass-word (păs′ wėrd) *n.* a secret word used for entrance

pas-ture (păs′ chėr) *n.* a grassy field where cattle and horses can graze

patch (păch) *n.* a small piece of cloth used to mend a hole

path-way (păth′ wā) *n.* a walkway

pa-tient-ly (pā′ shənt lē) *adv.* with calmness or the willingness to handle difficulties

paw (pô) *n.* the foot of an animal

peach (pēch) *n.* a fruit with a fuzzy skin

pear (pãr) *n.* a sweet fruit usually pointed at the stem and rounded at the bottom

pi-a-no (pē ăn′ ō) *n. pl.* **pi-a-nos** a musical instrument in which felt-covered hammers, operated from a keyboard, strike metal strings to make the sound.

pic-co-lo (pĭk′ ə lō) *n. pl.* **pic-co-los** a small flute that plays an octave higher than an ordinary flute

pi-rate (pī ′ rĭt) *n.* a person who robs ships at sea

plain (plān) 1. *n.* a flat area of land with no trees 2. *adj.* not fancy

plane (plān) *n.* an airplane

pleas-ant (plĕz′ ənt) *adj.* friendly; agreeable

pleas-ure (plĕzh′ ər) *n.* something that is enjoyable

point-ed (poin′ tĭd) *adj.* having a sharp end

police

po-lice (pə lēs′) *n.* officers of the law

po-lite (pə līt′) *adj.* having good manners

poo-dle (pü′ dəl) *n.* a dog with thick curly hair

pop-corn (pŏp′ cōrn) *n.* a kind of corn whose kernels burst open and puff out when they are heated

pop-u-lar (pŏp′ yə lėr) *adj.* well-liked

pork (pōrk) *n.* the flesh of hogs that is used for food

port-a-ble (pōr′ tə bəl) *adj.* something that can easily be carried

post-pone (pōst pōn′) *v.* to delay or put off doing something

po-ta-to (pə tā′ tō) *n. pl.* **po-ta-toes** a thick rounded, underground stem of a plant which is brown or red on the outside and white on the inside which is eaten as a vegetable

pre-cook (prē′ kůk) *v.* to cook beforehand

pre-judge (prē′ jŭdj) *v.* to make a decision without hearing all the facts

pre-paid (prē′ pād) *v.* to pay before something is due or before one receives a thing

recall

pro-cras-ti-nate (prō krăs′ tə nāt) *v.* to delay or put off action

pro-hib-it (prō hĭb′ ĭt) *v.* to forbid someone from doing something

pro-jec-tor (prō jĕk′ tėr) *n.* an apparatus for showing an enlarged image onto a screen

pur-chase (pėr′ chəs) *v.* to acquire by payment of money

pur-ple (pėr′ pəl) *n.* a color that is made by mixing red and blue

purse (pėrs) *n.* another name for a handbag

Q q

qui-et (kwī′ ət) *adj.* without noise

quo-ta-tion (kwō tā′ shən) *n.* the repeat of a person's exact words

R r

ra-di-o (rā′ dē ō) *n. pl.* **ra-di-os** a device used for sending or receiving waves of sound

re-al-i-ty (rē oul′ ĭ tē) *n. pl.* **re-al-i-ties** the state or quality of being real

re-call (rē′ kôl) *v.* to bring back to the mind ;to call back

receive

re-ceive (rĭ sēv′) *v.* to take or get

re-duc-i-ble (rĭ düs′ ə bəl) *adj.* able to be made smaller

reef (rēf) *n. pl.* **reefs** a ridge of rock or coral just below the surface of the water

re-frig-e-ra-tor (rĭ frĭj′ ə rā tėr) *n.* a machine used to keep food cool

re-gion (rē′ jən) *n.* a large part of a surface

re-pair (rĭ pãr′) *v.* to fix something

re-ply (rē plī ′) *n.* an answer

re-search (rē′ sėrch) *v.* to hunt for facts

re-serve (rĭ zėrv′) *v.* to save or keep back

re-trace (rē trās′) *v.* to go back over

re-turn (rē tėrn′) *v.* to take back or send back

re-vers-i-ble (rĭ vėr′ sə bəl) *adj.* able to be worn with either side out

re-write (rē′ rīt) *v.* to write again

rib-bon (rĭb′ ən) *n.* a long strip of cloth

roam (rōm) *v.* to wander; to go from place to place without a goal

scenario

roast (rōst) *v.* to cook meat in an oven or over a fire

roof (rüf) *n. pl.* **roofs** the outside upper cover of a building

round-ed (roun′ dĭd) *adj.* shaped like a circle; not pointed

S s

sa-lute (sə lüt′) 1. *n.* a sign made with the hand which shows respect or greeting
2. *v.* to give a salute

saw-dust (sô′ dŭst) *n.* flecks of ground-up wood

saw-mill (sô′ mĭl) *n.* a place where logs are cut

scap-u-la (skăp′ yū lə) *n.* the scientific name for the shoulder blade

scare-crow (skãr′ krō) *n.* a figure resembling a man, dressed in ragged clothes, used to scare birds from a garden

scar-let (skär′ lĭt) *n.* a bright red color tinged with orange

sce-nar-i-o (sĭ nãr′ ē ō) *n.*
pl. **sce-nar-i-os**
an outline of a play, containing directions about the scenes, characters, etc.

scene

scene (sēn) *n.* the place where some action has taken place

scen-er-y (sē′ nə rē) *n.* a grouping or arrangement of things in a large view

scent (sĭnt) *n.* an odor

sci-ence (sī ′ əns) *n.* the study or knowledge dealing with a group of facts arranged in an orderly fashion

sci-en-tif-ic (sī ′ ən tĭf ′ ĭk) *adj.* concerning, produced by, or used in science

sci-en-tist (sī ′ ən tĭst) *n.* a person who specializes in an area of science

sci-on (sī ′ ən) *n.* a shoot, sprout, bud, or twig that is grafted onto another plant

scis-sors (sĭz ′ ėrz) *n.* a tool used to cut things

scold (skōld) *v.* to criticize or blame angrily

scoot-er (skü t′ ėr) *n.* a child's vehicle made of metal or wood supported between two wheels and steered with an upright handlebar

scorch (skōrch) *v.* to burn lightly on the surface

shelter

scor-pi-on (skōr ′ pē ən) *n.* an animal, related to spiders, that looks like a lobster and has a poisonous sting at the end of its tail

scoun-drel (skoun ′ drəl) *n.* a mean or dishonorable person

scribe (skrīb) *n.* a person who works at writing or copying; a scholar and teacher of Jewish law0

search (sėrch) *v.* to look for something

sea-shore (sē′ shōr) *n.* the edge along the ocean

sent (sĭnt) *v.* did send

serv-ant (sėr′ vənt) *n.* a person employed to serve or wait on another

ser-vice (sėr′ vəs) *n.* work performed for another person, group, or organization

shal-low (shoul′ ō) *adj.* not deep

sharp (shärp) *adj.* having a fine edge

sheep (shēp) *n. pl.* **sheep** an animal related to the goat whose hair is used for wool

shel-ter (shĕl′ tėr) *n.* a place that protects from weather or danger

shiver

shiv-er (shĭv′ ėr) *v.* to shake with cold or fear

short-en (shōrt′ ən) *v.* to make smaller, to cut off

shout (shout) *v.* to say or utter something very loudly

shove (shəv) *v.* move something with force: to push somebody or something along or forward with force

shrimp (shrĭmp) *n.* a small, mainly ocean-dwelling crustacean with ten legs

shrink (shrĭngk) *v.* to make or become smaller

si-lence (sī′ ləns) *n.* a quietness; a lack of noise

sim-i-lar (sĭm′ ə lėr) *adj.* alike

sim-ple (sĭm′ pəl) *adj.* easy to do

sky-ward (skī ′ wėrd) *adj.* heading toward the sky

sleigh (slā) *n.* horse-drawn carriage used on snow

slight (slīt) *adj.* small; unimportant

slip-per (slĭp′ ėr) *n.* a light, low shoe

sneeze (snēz) *v.* to blow air through the nose without being able to stop it

staff

sole (sōl) *n.* the bottom of a foot or shoe

sought (sôt) *v.* the past tense of seek

soul (sōl) *n.* the inner being of a person

spa-ghet-ti (spə gĕt′ ē) *n.* string-shaped pasta: pasta in the shape of long thin strings

spare (spãr) 1. *v.* refrain from harming someone 2. *n.* an extra

spark (spärk) *n.* a small bit of fire

spe-cial (spĕsh′ əl) *adj.* of a distinct particular kind

spi-der (spī′ dėr) *n.* an animal that spins a web and can go anywhere

spin-ach (spĭn′ ĭch *n. pl.* **spinach** an annual plant widely cultivated for its edible dark green leaves

sprain (sprān) *v.* to hurt a part of the body by twisting it too far

spy (spī) *n.* a person who secretly watches another person

sta-ble (stā′ bəl) *n.* a building where horses or cattle are kept

staff (stăf) *n. pl.* **staffs** a particular group of employees within a company, institution, or organization

station

sta-tion (stā′ shən) *n.* a stopping place for trains and buses [From Latin *statio*, a standing still]

stee-ple (stē′ pəl) *n.* a church tower

stew (stü) *n.* a thick mixture of meat and vegetables that are boiled together slowly

stretch (strĕch) *v.* to draw out; extend [From Middle English *strecchen*, to spread out]

stu-dent (stüd′ ənt) *n.* a person who is studying

stu-di-o (stü′ dē ō) *n.* a place from which radio and television shows can be broadcasted

style (stīl) . *n.* fashion

sub-ma-rine (sŭb′ mə rēn) *n.* a warship able to travel underwater

sub-merge (sŭb mėrj′) *v.* to sink or plunge beneath the surface of the water

sub-way (sŭb′ wā) *n.* an underground electric railroad

suit-case (süt′ kās) *n.* a traveling bag for clothing

sup-port (sə pōrt′) *v.* to bear or hold up

title

surf-board (sėrf ′ bōrd) *n.* a long board used to ride ocean waves

sword (sōrd) *n.* a weapon with a long, short blade

T t

tal-ent (toul′ ənt) *n.* a natural ability or skill

tar-get (tär′ gĭt) *n.* a goal for shooting

teach-er (tēch′ ėr) *n.* a person who teaches

tease (tēz) *v.* to upset by playing tricks

they (thā) *pron.* the people or things already mentioned or identified, or understood by both the speaker and hearer

thick-en (thĭk′ ən) *v.* to make thick

thief (thēf) *pl.* **thieves** a person who steals

thir-teen (thėr′ tēn) *n. adj.* one more than twelve

thrown (thrōn) *v.* the past tense of throw

ti-tle (tī ′ təl) *n.* the name of a book, poem, or song

tomato

to‑ma‑to (tə mā′ tō) *n. pl.* **to‑ma‑toes** a round red or yellow smooth-skinned fruit

tongue (tŭng) *n.* the movable fleshy organ attached to the bottom of the inside of the mouth

tooth (tüth) *n. pl.* **teeth** any of the hard, white bony parts growing from the jaws and used to bite or chew

tor‑na‑do (tōr nā′ dō) *n. pl.* **tor‑na‑does** a violent wind storm in which winds form a funnel-shaped cloud and cause great destruction

to‑tal (tō′ təl) 1. *n.* a sum of all parts 2. *v.* to add up all the parts of something

town (toun) *n.* a village
town's *possessive of one town*
towns' *possessive of more than one town*

treas‑ure (trĕzh′ ėr) 1. *n.* anything of value 2. *v.* to value something

tri‑an‑gle (trī ′ ăng gəl) *n.* a shape with three sides and three angles

trout (trout) *n.* a freshwater fish that is typically smaller than the related salmon and has a speckled body, small scales, and soft fins

truth (trüth) *n.* what is true or real

vitamin

tune (tün) *n.* a melody; a selection of music

type (tīp) *v.* to write with a machine

U u

un‑beat‑a‑ble (ŭn bēt′ ə bəl) *adj.* not able to be beaten

un‑cov‑er (ŭn kŭv′ ėr) *v.* to take the cover off

un‑der‑ground (ŭn dėr ground′) *adj.* beneath the surface of the ground

u‑ni‑form (yū′ nə fōrm) *n.* a distinctive set of clothes worn to identify somebody's occupation, affiliation, or status

un‑kind (ŭn kīnd′) *adj.* not kind

u‑su‑al (yū′ zhū əl) *adj.* expected or customary

V v

verse (vėrs) *n.* one of the lines of a poem

vis‑i‑ble (vĭz′ ə bəl) *adj.* able to be seen

vi‑ta‑min (vī′ tə mĭn) *n.* any of a group of organic substances necessary for the health of the body

W w

waist (wāst) *n.* the narrow part of the human body between the ribs and the hips

wait (wāt) *v.* to hold oneself ready for an event

wash-a-ble (wŏsh ′ ə bəl) *adj.* capable of being washed

waste (wāst) *v.* to consume; to employ uselessly or without good return

wear-ing (wãr′ ĭng) *v.* to have on one's body as a covering

wea-ry (wēr′ ē) *adj.* physically or mentally exhausted

weight (wāt) *n.* the heaviness of an object or person

west (wĕst) 1. *n.* the direction in which the sun sets 2. *adj.* in or from the west

wheat (wēt) *n.* the grain in various cereal grasses used in making flour

whis-per (hwĭs ′ pėr) *v.* to speak softly

won-der (wŭn′ dėr) *v.* to think about; to want to know

Y y

year-ling (yēr ′ lĭng) *n.* an animal between one and two years old

yearn (yėrn) *v.* to long for; to have a strong desire for

young (yŭng) *adj.* not old; in the early years of life

Z z

zone (zōn) *n.* a certain geographical area

zuc-chi-ni (zü kē′ nē) *n.* a small summer squash that is shaped like a cucumber

Unit 6
Part 1

Circle the letter of the correct spelling of the word.

1. A _____ train derailed and exploded.

    A. freght   B. freight   C. frate

2. Amanda was our _____.

    A. neighbor   B. neighbour   C. naighbor

3. A _____ would be handy to pick up a car.

    A. craen   B. crane   C. cranne

4. Almanzo Wilder wanted to take Laura for a ride on a _____.

    A. slaigh   B. sliegh   C. sleigh

5. Practice your piano lesson _____.

    A. daily   B. daley   C. dialy

6. We _____ Thanksgiving with a big meal.

    A. selebrate   B. cellebrate   C. celebrate

7. Would you like to take a _____ hike?

    A. natere   B. nature   C. nachur

8. Bread is made from _____.

    A. grane   B. grein   C. grain

9. There are not _____ days in one week.

    A. eight   B. eiight   C. eaght

10. Do not try to _____ your answer.

    A. irase   B. erase   C. eraes

11. You should _____ those that have the rule over you.

    A. obay   B. obey   C. obeiy

12. I called the _____ because of the drunk driver.

    A. police   B. polece   C. pulease

13. Andrew was _____ years old.

    A. ninteen   B. ninetean   C. nineteen

14. Can you find a _____ pack of candy bars?

    A. jumboe   B. jambo   C. jumbo

15. The people owned a black _____.

    A. poodel   B. poodle   C. poudle

16. I did not want the job situation to become a _____ issue.

    A. leigal   B. legel   C. legal

17. I wanted to take a _____ C.

    A. vitamen   B. vitumin   C. vitamin

18. What was our _____ sales at the flea market?

    A. total   B. toetal   C. totel

19. Mara had a _____ tooth.

    A. louse   B. loose   C. lose

20. I do not want to be sick with a _____.

    A. fever   B. fevur   C. feaver

21. Learning to _____ by fives should be easy.

    A. multeply   B. maltiply   C. multiply

22. James went to the _____ Wednesday morning.

    A. grocery   B. grosery   C. growcery

23. David wanted to give us a _____ of what he was talking about.

    A. cloeu   B. clew   C. clue

24. Did he _____ the task?

    A. cumplete   B. complete   C. compleat

25. I did not hear his first _____ to my question.

    A. reply   B. riply   C. repply

Unit 6
Part 2

Circle the letter of the correct spelling of the word.

1. Did you measure the _____ of the tree?

    A. groeth			B. groath			C. growth

2. Frankie made some _____.

    A. stew			B. stoew			C. stoow

3. James painted the bathroom _____.

    A. cieling			B. ceiling			C. cealing

4. Ben said he had a _____.

    A. spieder			B. spider			C. spidur

5. We walked into the portrait _____

    A. stuedio			B. studeo			C. studio

6. I let the dentist pull my _____.

    A. touth			B. toeth			C. tooth

7. I _____ I have gained weight.

    A. believe			B. beleive			C. beleave

8. I rode a pink _____.

    A. bisycle			B. bicycle			C. bicycel

9. I did not want to _____ making the tests.

    A. postpone			B. postpoan			C. postepone

10. Do you know the _____ to a patriotic song?

    A. toon   B. tune   C. tunne

11. I poured _____ into the jar.

    A. greace   B. greese   C. grease

12. Do not stay outside when there is _____.

    A. lighting   B. lightning   C. lightneng

13. Mother fixed a _____.

    A. roast   B. roest   C. roste

14. I hope I do not make a _____ mistake.

    A. fullish   B. foolesh   C. foolish

15. _____ Massosoit was friendly to the pilgrims.

    A. Chief   B. Cheif   C. Chefe

16. Was the Lusitania a _____ ship?

    A. pyrate   B. pirate   C. pirete

17. A snake can hide in a _____ log.

    A. holow   B. hollow   C. holloe

18. Please stand and _____ the flag.

    A. sulute   B. saloot   C. salute

19. Richard cooked enough food for a Thanksgiving _____.

    A. feast   B. feest   C. feist

20. What _____ of blood do you have?

    A. tipe   B. type   C. typpe

21. I put _____ on my hands.

    A. loition   B. loetion   C. lotion

22. Always tell the _____.

    A. trouth   B. truth   C. trueth

23. Hepatitis is a liver _____.

    A. disease   B. diseace   C. dizease

24. There was _____ in the room.

    A. silence   B. silince   C. silense

25. Did you _____ my keys?

    A. loacate   B. lokate   C. locate

Unit 6
Part 3

Circle the letter of the correct spelling of the word.

1. A _____ of people from Hodgenville were on the bus.

    A. group   B. groap   C. gruep

2. The church's _____ was tall.

    A. steaple   B. steeple   C. steepel

3. It might be fun to be a _____.

    A. spy   B. spie   C. spye

4. Have you _____ the newspaper away?

    A. throan   B. throen   C. thrown

5. Byron was born in _____.

    A. Juen   B. Joune   C. June

6. We should try to be happy and not _____.

    A. complane   B. complain   C. complein

7. I was not trying to _____ the woman.

    A. displeaze   B. displease   C. displeese

8. I want an interesting _____ for my story.

    A. title   B. tittle   C. titel

9. _____ your attention on the speaker.

    A. Foecus   B. Fokus   C. Focus

10. The wind _____ hard against the van.

    A. blew   B. blue   C. bloe

11. Did Anthony _____ his ankle?

    A. sprane   B. sprain   C. spraen

12. Put your shoes _____ the chair.

    A. beneath   B. beneeth   C. beneith

13. _____ the cake into eight pieces.

    A. Divied   B. Divide   C. Devide

14. To write the speaker's exact words is a _____.

    A. quotashun   B. quoetation   C. quotation

15. An apple is a _____.

    A. friut   B. frout   C. fruit

16. Have _____ in God.

    A. faeth   B. faith   C. fiath

17. A foundation should be made of _____.

    A. concrete   B. concreate   C. concreat

18. I tried to be _____.

    A. polight   B. polite   C. poliet

19. To _____ through the woods might be peaceful.

    A. roem   B. rome   C. roam

20. The _____ was packed for their visit.

    A. suetcase   B. suitcase   C. siutcase

Unit 6
Part 4

Circle the letter of the correct spelling of the word.

1. I wanted my students to _____ on a field trip.

    A. behaeve   B. bihave   C. behave

2. A _____ is a fuzzy fruit.

    A. peech   B. peach   C. peich

3. There was a _____ difference in the color of the yarn.

    A. slite   B. slyght   C. slight

4. I did not know how to shoot the _____.

    A. airow   B. arrow   C. arow

5. Have you ever ridden in a _____?

    A. canoe   B. canou   C. cunoe

6. Sit down and let the photographer _____ your picture.

    A. retake   B. retaek   C. ritake

7. Are the schools _____ closed?

    A. indead   B. indeed   C. endeed

8. Have you ever made a cake shaped like a _____?

    A. triangle   B. triangel   C. trianngel

9. The orchard had a _____ of trees.

    A. groave   B. grove   C. groav

253

10. I don't believe all of the Titanic's _____ got off safely.

   A. croe   B. croo   C. crew

11. _____ were back soon.

   A. Thay   B. Thaye   C. They

12. _____ James nor I want a dog for a pet.

   A. Neither   B. Niether   C. Neather

13. I had _____ dollars in the paper clip.

   A. ninty   B. ninety   C. nienty

14. We could have _____ decorations if it were our fiftieth anniversary.

   A. golden   B. goldun   C. goelden

15. Teri wanted to _____ me to her friend.

   A. entroduce   B. interduce   C. introduce

16. Frankie had an _____ in his head.

   A. ake   B. ache   C. aeche

17. Did he _____ the note that was mailed?

   A. recieve   B. receive   C. riceive

18. Is that shirt out of _____ ?

   A. style   B. stile   C. stiele

19. There was a _____ part of the pool.

   A. shollow   B. shalloe   C. shallow

20. It is a teacher's _____ to help students learn.

   A. douty   B. dutie   C. duty

Unit 12
Part 1

Circle the letter of the correct spelling of the word.

1. If I were a _____, I'd help a lot of people.

   A. millionair B. milionaire C. millionaire

2. Jimmy had _____ hair.

   A. curly B. cerly C. curley

3. Jesus fasted for _____ days.

   A. forrty B. forty C. fourty

4. Some dogs have three _____.

   A. paws B. pause C. pauze

5. A _____ sheet would be warm.

   A. flanel B. flannel C. flannell

6. Lee had his own _____.

   A. apartmant B. apartmint C. apartment

7. We went on a long _____ to Florida.

   A. jerney B. jorney C. journey

8. David used Goliath's own _____ to kill him.

   A. sword B. sord C. swurd

9. What is the _____ of his illness?

   A. couse B. cause C. cauze

10. Where was one blue _____?

    A. sliper   B. slipper   C. clippar

11. The Titanic never made it to the New York _____.

    A. harbor   B. harbour   C. harbar

12. The _____ had a lot of compartments.

    A. purce   B. purrse   C. purse

13. The Ohio River forms the _____ border of Kentucky.

    A. northern   B. northurn   C. northirn

14. Kevin owned a blue _____.

    A. awtomobile   B. automobile   C. automobill

15. Have you ever seen a real _____?

    A. alligater   B. aligator   C. alligator

16. One little _____ might burn you.

    A. sperk   B. spark   C. sparek

17. I do not want to _____ myself while riding a bike.

    A. injure   B. injere   C. injur

18. Bacon is _____ meat.

    A. porke   B. pork   C. pourk

19. Who _____ the chili?

    A. brought   B. brote   C. brouht

20. Teachers should use proper _____.

    A. gramar   B. grammer   C. grammar

21. Did Brenda walk _____ than Rebecca?

    A. ferther   B. farthur   C. farther

22. The _____ of Byron was earlier than we expected.

    A. birth   B. berth   C. burth

23. The planets _____ around the sun.

    A. orbiit   B. orbit   C. orbite

24. There was _____ on the ground under the tent.

    A. sawdust   B. saudust   C. sowdust

25. Benjamin acts _____ to the way Jimmy did.

    A. simelar   B. similar   C. similer

Unit 12
Part 2

Circle the letter of the correct spelling of the word.

1. I paid for a _____ call for the air conditioner.

    A. sirvice B. service C. servuce

2. The fire _____ sounds if there is a tornado warning.

    A. alram B. allarm C. alarm

3. How much _____ is needed to lift a car?

    A. force B. forse C. forsse

4. Mike likes to get paid to _____ junk.

    A. hawl B. hauol C. haul

5. The homeless _____ used to be a school.

    A. shellter B. shelter C. sheltar

6. Which _____ do you prefer to use when flying?

    A. airrline B. airline C. areline

7. Carolyn was the _____ for our precinct.

    A. clerk B. clirk C. clurk

8. Did you ever pick apples from his _____?

    A. orcherd B. orchard C. orchurd

9. You _____ to obey your parents.

    A. ought B. aught C. owght

10. The election in November 2012 was a _____ election.

    A. mejor   B. magor   C. major

11. Frankie might not know how to _____ some cars.

    A. repare   B. repear   C. repair

12. Riding on a _____ can be dangerous.

    A. surfboard   B. serfboard   C. surfbored

13. You might find a bear if you _____ a cave in winter.

    A. eksplore   B. explore   C. explour

14. I have an _____ washing machine.

    A. awtomatic   B. automatick   C. automatic

15. I thought there was a fall _____ in Fairdale a long time ago.

    A. festivul   B. festaval   C. festival

16. It takes a lot of work to clean an _____.

    A. aqwarium   B. aquarium   C. aquareum

17. Have you put _____ into the washer?

    A. detergent   B. deterjent   C. detirgent

18. You could hem the pants to _____ them.

    A. shorten   B. shortin   C. shorrten

19. Paul said he had _____ a good fight.

    A. faught   B. fawght   C. fought

20. Frankfort is the _____ of Kentucky.

    A. capittal   B. capital   C. cappital

21. James wanted to have a _____ tire before taking the trailer.

    A. spare   B. spair   C. sparre

22. I made two _____ dresses.

    A. purpal   B. pirple   C. purple

23. Tennessee is on the southern _____ of Kentucky.

    A. bordar   B. border   C. borrder

24. I have a lot of _____ to do after vacation.

    A. laundry   B. lawndry   C. londry

25. Does James have a _____?

    A. chizel   B. chicel   C. chisel

Unit 12
Part 3

Circle the letter of the correct spelling of the word.

1. Was it a _____ ship that sunk?

   A. cargo   B. carego   C. carggo

2. Wendy is older than _____ years old.

   A. thurteen   B. thirtean   C. thirteen

3. I had an old _____ radio.

   A. portable   B. portabel   C. purtable

4. _____ I wanted chicken, we went to the restaurant.

   A. Becawse   B. Because   C. Becuse

5. We visited Lee in the _____.

   A. hospetal   B. hospital   C. hospitle

6. Did you hit a _____ with an arrow?

   A. targit   B. tarrget   C. target

7. We did some _____ on Alzheimer's disease.

   A. research   B. riserch   C. reserch

8. I did not want to choose a speaker that would _____ everyone.

   A. boar   B. borre   C. bore

9. I _____ some shirts at the store.

   A. baught   B. bought   C. bowght

263

10. I do not like for children to _____ their food in the floor.

    A. crumbel   B. crumble   C. crummble

11. Do not try to _____ two children from the same family.

    A. compair   B. cumpare   C. compare

12. I was trying to memorize the second _____.

    A. verse   B. verze   C. verce

13. It is good for children to learn to do some _____.

    A. chorres   B. chores   C. choores

14. Leaves fall from most trees in the _____ season.

    A. awtume   B. autumm   C. autumn

15. Turn right at the next _____.

    A. corrner   B. cornur   C. corner

16. It is easier to control a dog if you use a _____.

    A. harniss   B. harness   C. harnuss

17. Do not turn the _____; just pull into the driveway.

    A. curve   B. cerve   C. curv

18. Would it be _____ to have a woman president for the United States?

    A. normle   B. normel   C. normal

19. Would you include the _____ of the book in a book report?

    A. awthor   B. author   C. auther

20. Please put a _____ on every dish we take.

    A. label   B. lable   C. labbel

Unit 12
Part 4

Circle the letter of the correct spelling of the word.

1. Do not be _____ when standing on a ladder.

    A. careliss	B. carless	C. careless

2. I can _____ for another bicycle.

    A. serch	B. search	C. saerch

3. Jesus taught people while they stood on the _____.

    A. seashore	B. seeshore	C. seashure

4. Frankie looked like he felt _____.

    A. auful	B. awfull	C. awful

5. James built a _____ for the nativity set.

    A. stable	B. stabel	C. staeble

6. I wish Charles could get a _____.

    A. paredon	B. pardun	C. pardon

7. I do not want a pinched _____ in my back.

    A. nurve	B. nerve	C. neerve

8. Jesus was not an _____ man.

    A. ordenary	B. ordinairy	C. ordinary

9. James gets _____ drops to help his throat feel better.

    A. cough	B. coff	C. coagh

10. A _____ is used when riding a horse.

    A. bridel   B. bridle   C. briddel

11. It is not good to _____ with people.

    A. argeu   B. argue   C. aregue

12. I did not want Joyce to _____ with James.

    A. flirt   B. flert   C. flurt

13. Would you _____ him to get his driver's license?

    A. forbid   B. forebid   C. forbide

14. The man sold oak wood from his _____.

    A. saumill   B. sawmell   C. sawmill

15. I am not a very _____ pianist.

    A. popelar   B. popular   C. popalar

16. A _____ is lit by some wrecks if they occur at night time.

    A. flair   B. flaer   C. flare

17. The newborn baby looked very _____ in the picture.

    A. alirt   B. alert   C. alurt

18. He poured concrete to help _____ the weight of the deck.

    A. support   B. suport   C. suppurt

19. We _____ for the keys.

    A. saught   B. sowght   C. sought

20. A _____ has the same value as five pennies.

    A. nickel   B. nickle   C. nikel

Unit 18
Part 1

Circle the letter of the correct spelling of the word.

1. Kevin was an _____ welder.

   A. exsellent   B. ekcellent   C. excellent

2. Always use sharp _____ when cutting fabric.

   A. scizors   B. scissors   C. scissores

3. Make sure you _____ the test.

   A. finich   B. finnish   C. finish

4. The wedding dress was _____.

   A. beautiful   B. beutiful   C. beautifull

5. I bit my _____.

   A. tongue   B. tounge   C. toungue

6. I would not want to fight a _____.

   A. goerilla   B. gorilla   C. gorila

7. It was a _____ to work with the officials.

   A. pleasure   B. plesure   C. pleazhure

8. I like to use a food _____.

   A. choper   B. chopper   C. choppar

9. Would you want a house made of _____ bricks?

   A. adobee   B. adoebe   C. adobe

10. I did not mean to _____ her down.

    A. shuve   B. shuv   C. shove

11. Robbie enjoyed riding a _____.

    A. motocycle   B. motorcycle   C. motorcycel

12. It is an inconvenience to _____ the van key.

    A. lose   B. loose   C. loze

13. One-third is a large _____.

    A. fracsion   B. fraccion   C. fraction

14. He drove halfway _____ the town square.

    A. arownd   B. around   C. arouned

15. Please do not leave the _____ in the floor.

    A. glove   B. gluve   C. glave

16. We live in a small _____.

    A. citty   B. sity   C. city

17. Our street is not the _____ in our town.

    A. busiest   B. busyest   C. bisiest

18. He could bend metal to make a _____.

    A. chanel   B. channel   C. channal

19. I got some milk from the _____.

    A. refrijerator   B. refrigerator   C. refrigeratar

20. Will you loan me a _____ of dollars?

    A. cuple   B. coupel   C. couple

21. Some people accuse others of _____ people.

    A. judging   B. judgeing   C. judjing

22. My brothers liked to _____ me when I was young.

    A. teaze   B. tease   C. teese

23. Did you think the piano was _____?

    A. anciant   B. antient   C. ancient

24. There was a lot of noise in the _____.

    A. cafateria   B. cafeteria   C. cafeterea

25. I do not know what the _____ of America will be.

    A. future   B. fewture   C. fucher

Unit 18
Part 2

Circle the letter of the correct spelling of the word.

1. Matthew passed the _____ test.

    A. geometry	B. geomatry	C. geemoetry

2. I should _____ if I want to lose weight.

    A. exerzise	B. exercise	C. exersise

3. I do not want to _____ deep into a cave.

    A. addventure	B. advinture	C. adventure

4. Robbie is my second _____.

    A. couzin	B. cousin	C. cuosin

5. We could clear the road of snow if it were a _____ effort.

    A. comunity	B. communety	C. community

6. In what _____ of North America do you live?

    A. rejion	B. region	C. regiun

7. I like to eat _____ and crackers.

    A. cheze	B. cheese	C. cheeze

8. It is _____ for babies to love their mothers.

    A. natural	B. natchural	C. naturel

9. We could have settled in a _____ if we lived in the 1700s.

    A. colany	B. collony	C. colony

271

10. James and Kevin worked for the same _____ .

    A. company   B. cumpany   C. comepany

11. There is a small _____ at the end of the road.

    A. gazebo   B. gasebo   C. gazeboe

12. I tried to _____ the ribbon.

    A. meazure   B. mesure   C. measure

13. I felt like I had been _____ waiting for an answer to my email.

    A. pashently   B. patiently   C. paciently

14. We _____ arrived home.

    A. finally   B. finnaly   C. finaly

15. I _____ what will happen to America.

    A. wunder   B. wonder   C. wander

16. Try to _____ the correct answer.

    A. gess   B. geuss   C. guess

17. Sometimes I read the little _____ .

    A. maguzine   B. magasine   C. magazine

18. I have seen the Atlantic _____ .

    A. Ocean   B. Osean   C. Oceen

19. I am _____ tired.

    A. sertainly   B. certainly   C. certenly

20. I saw the truck _____ rock into our driveway.

    A. doump   B. dummp   C. dump

21. I do not want to be in the middle of a _____.

    A. cyclone   B. ciclone   C. syclone

22. It is _____ for brothers to be able to get along instead of fighting.

    A. pleasant   B. plezant   C. pleazant

23. Goliath thought he would be the _____.

    A. chumpion   B. champeon   C. champion

24. Can you find a _____ in which we could store things?

    A. barel   B. barrel   C. barrle

25. You may be _____ from the table if you are sick.

    A. escused   B. excused   C. excuesed

Unit 18
Part 3

Circle the letter of the correct spelling of the word.

1. _____ plants can live in a desert.

    A. Cacktus B. Cactas C. Cactus

2. It was very _____ that the little boy's face was dirty.

    A. visible B. vizible C. visable

3. There were many cows in the _____.

    A. paschure B. pasture C. pastur

4. Driving in fog makes it difficult to see _____.

    A. afare B. afire C. afar

5. My mother lived on Morgan _____ for a long time.

    A. Avenue B. Avanue C. Avenew

6. We could _____ to take the children out to eat.

    A. arange B. arranje C. arrange

7. You can _____ a room in a motel if you want.

    A. rezerve B. reserve C. resurve

8. If a lion gets loose from the zoo, I hope they _____ it quickly.

    A. captire B. capture C. capshure

9. No _____ was to be at school before 8:30 A.M.

    A. student B. studant C. studint

10. _____ of us want it to snow in November.

    A. Nune   B. None   C. Nun

11. Benjamin was not willing to _____ a hamburger.

    A. cunsume   B. consoome   C. consume

12. The Bible should be like a _____ to us.

    A. treasure   B. treazhure   C. tresure

13. I wanted to try to _____ the jumper instead of throw it away.

    A. patch   B. pach   C. patche

14. I found the perfect _____ for the little girls' jumpers.

    A. ribbun   B. ribbon   C. ribon

15. Do you want a _____ put on the pants?

    A. caff   B. couff   C. cuff

16. The Rotunda Room was in a _____ shape.

    A. curcular   B. circular   C. circuler

17. Make sure you get a tissue if you feel like you are going to _____.

    A. sneaze   B. sneese   C. sneeze

18. Veteran's Day is a _____ holiday to remember Veterans.

    A. specual   B. special   C. spetial

19. I wish Donna did not live such a great _____ from us.

    A. distance   B. distunce   C. destance

20. _____ people usually have more energy that elderly people.

    A. Youing   B. Yung   C. Young

Unit 18
Part 4

Circle the letter of the correct spelling of the word.

1. I would like to have a big _____ for our school.

    A. gymnazium	B. gymnasium	C. gymasium

2. It is a _____ feeling to have a migraine headache.

    A. miserable	B. mizerable	C. miserabel

3. We went to the train _____ early in the morning.

    A. stacion	B. stattion	C. station

4. Teresa has a wonderful _____ for playing the guitar.

    A. talunt	B. talent	C. talant

5. Doyle did not order a _____ to wear to work.

    A. unniform	B. unaform	C. uniform

6. Most schools begin in the month of _____.

    A. August	B. Awgust	C. Augest

7. We were busy like a _____ presidential election.

    A. uzual	B. usual	C. usuel

8. Richard made _____ for people to sit on in his church.

    A. binches	B. benchs	C. benches

9. Would you like to teach in an _____ school?

    A. elamentary	B. elementery	C. elementary

10. A gorilla is not _____.

    A. human   B. humane   C. hueman

11. James swirled the _____ in our bathroom.

    A. seiling   B. ceiling   C. cieling

12. The people, flying in a balloon, were glad to be out of the _____.

    A. zoene   B. zone   C. zoan

13. It is easy to _____ if you're outside on a very cold morning.

    A. shivir   B. shivar   C. shiver

14. It is not _____ to yell in the classroom.

    A. necessary   B. nesessary   C. necesary

15. Don't _____ the blocks in the container.

    A. jumble   B. jumbel   C. jambel

16. Always treat a _____ right if you want them to come back.

    A. custamer   B. customer   C. customre

17. Lynn was _____ to be on the jury.

    A. chozen   B. chosin   C. chosen

18. A woman should not have _____ hair.

    A. fasial   B. faciel   C. facial

19. The young couple were willing to _____ a child.

    A. adopt   B. addopt   C. adoppt

20. Stay within your _____ if you don't want to be in debt.

    A. budjet   B. budget   C. budgit

Unit 24
Part 1

Circle the letter of the correct spelling of the word.

1. We should never speak _____ words to people.

    A. unkiend   B. unkinde   C. unkind

2. Frankie was very _____.

    A. malnourished   B. malnerished   C. molnourished

3. Did Britain _____ goods to America?

    A. eksport   B. export   C. expoart

4. Clarence was an _____ of the steel company.

    A. employea   B. employee   C. emploiee

5. I have _____ that he will tell me the truth.

    A. confidense   B. confedence   C. confidence

6. Do not drink _____ water.

    A. impure   B. empure   C. impuer

7. Jurors should not _____ before hearing the witnesses.

    A. perjudge   B. prejudge   C. prejudje

8. A _____ is a boat that goes underwater.

    A. submarine   B. submarene   C. submerine

9. The balloons headed _____.

    A. skywerd   B. skiward   C. skyward

10. It is _____ to walk on an icy pond if the temperature is above freezing.

    A. dangerus   B. danjerous   C. dangerous

11. Please be careful to not _____ words on a test.

    A. misspell   B. mispell   C. misppell

12. The tuition should be _____.

    A. prepayd   B. perpaid   C. prepaid

13. The defendants should _____ with the judge.

    A. coperate   B. cooperate   C coopirate

14. Karen had a job as a teacher's _____.

    A. assistant   B. asistant   C. assistent

15. What is the _____ of the case?

    A. legalety   B. legality   C. leggality

16. I _____ of Zach moving out of the house.

    A. disaprove   B. disaprov   C. disapprove

17. I believe he flew on a _____ flight to Florida.

    A. nunstop   B. nonstop   C. nonsstop

18. Joseph was a _____ to Potiphar.

    A. servant   B. sirvant   C. servent

19. I did not think I was very _____.

    A. createve   B. creative   C. creetive

20. Greg and I _____ on a few things.

    A. dissagree   B. disaggree   C. disagree

21. _____ milk, eggs, and cinnamon to make French toast.

    A. Cumbine   B. Combien   C. Combine

22. Always listen closely to your _____.

    A. teacher   B. teecher   C. teachur

23. I want to be considered a _____ person.

    A. depindable   B. dependable   C. dependabel

Unit 24
Part 2

Circle the letter of the correct spelling of the word.

1. The pain in my side caused me _____.

    A. discomfert	B. discomfort	C. discumfort

2. The _____ was seventy-six years old.

    A. auctioneer	B. awctioneer	C. auctionear

3. There was a _____ stream of water flowing from the faucet.

    A. continuos	B. continuous	C. contenuous

4. Did you have an _____ heart beat?

    A. iregular	B. irreguler	C. irregular

5. I used to _____ potatoes before I put them in a pot pie.

    A. precook	B. percook	C. precock

6. I would like to go to bed before _____.

    A. middnight	B. midnite	C. midnight

7. William voted by _____ ballot.

    A. abbsentee	B. absintee	C. absentee

8. I called the office to make an _____.

    A. apointment	B. appointment	C. appointmint

9. Do you believe the team is _____?

    A. unbeatable	B. unbeetable	C. unbeatabel

283

10. Should we _____ the Constitution?

    A. rewrite   B. rerite   C. rewriet

11. I hope to _____ people to live right.

    A. cumpel   B. compell   C. compel

12. The cold temperature caused the fudge to _____.

    A. hardin   B. harden   C. hardden

13. The judge's words were _____.

    A. impresive   B. impressive   C. impresseve

14. Is Mr. Obama _____ of lowering the debt?

    A. incapable   B. incappable   C. incapabel

15. I would like to _____ his actions.

    A. prohibbit   B. prohibet   C. prohibit

16. Many people _____ gifts at Christmas time.

    A. exchange   B. exchaeng   C. exchanje

17. The fiftieth anniversary is called the _____ one.

    A. goldan   B. golden   C. gollden

18. It takes a _____ man to run for president.

    A. curageous   B. courageous   C. couragous

19. It is _____ for people to fly without a machine.

    A. impossable   B. imposible   C. impossible

20. We should never _____ a man who has fought for our country.

   A. maltreat   B. maltreet   C. malltreat

21. How many _____ does a play need?

   A. codirecters   B. codirectors   C. codirecktors

22. The _____ was expensive.

   A. projecter   B. projectur   C. projector

23. There was not an _____ of his election from many people.

   A. acceptance   B. aceptance   C. acceptence

Unit 24
Part 3

Circle the letter of the correct spelling of the word.

1. Many boys like to _____.

   A. misbehave   B. missbehave   C. misbeehave

2. Dinosaurs are considered _____ today.

   A. nonliveing   B. nonliving   C. nunliving

3. Some nations may _____ against the United States.

   A. cunspire   B. conspierre   C. conspire

4. Sir Isaac Newton was a famous _____.

   A. sientist   B. scientest   C. scientist

5. Healing a blind man is a _____ thing.

   A. marvelous   B. marvalous   C. marvelus

6. It was a _____ for the reporter to yell his question.

   A. discourtesy   B. discurtesy   C. discourtisy

7. Some people think it is _____ for states to secede from the United States.

   A. nonsence   B. nonsense   C. nonsince

8. Did the president _____ the information?

   A. conseal   B. conceal   C. conceil

9. James was driving _____ in the van.

   A. backword   B. backwerd   C. backward

287

10. It is of great _____ to elect the right person.

    A. importance   B. importence   C. importanse

11. We should not _____ our parents.

    A. dishonour   B. dishoner   C. dishonor

12. Did the reporter try to _____ the president with his question?

    A. entangel   B. entangle   C. entengle

13. I did not _____ the mother's tardiness.

    A. excuse   B. exquse   C. excuze

14. Billy is a _____ in his own kitchen.

    A. bakor   B. bakker   C. baker

15. We should not depend on the _____ for everything.

    A. govirnment   B. governmint   C. government

16. The volcano had been _____ for many years.

    A. inaktive   B. inactive   C. inacttive

17. You can _____ the picture if you want.

    A. enlarge   B. emlarge   C. enlarje

18. You could be a _____ of the book with me.

    A. coeauthor   B. coawthor   C. coauthor

19. I do not want to be a _____.

    A. novulist   B. novelist   C. novelest

20. The dress is _____.

    A. washable   B. wushable   C. washabel

Unit 24
Part 4

Circle the letter of the correct spelling of the word.

1. I hope no one will _____ me to a different building.

    A. misdirect   B. missdirect   C. misderect

2. God wants to _____ us with His grace.

    A. inrich   B. enrech   C. enrich

3. If you will _____ all the facts, the criminal might be found.

    A. compiel   B. compile   C. commpile

4. Wasn't Ronald Reagan an _____ before he became president?

    A. acter   B. actor   C. acttor

5. Some jackets are made to be _____.

    A. reversable   B. reverssible   C. reversible

6. Listen closely so you will not _____ the rules.

    A. missunderstand   B. misundarstand   C. misunderstand

7. I am a _____ of Bullitt County.

    A. nonresident   B. nonrezident   C. nonresidant

8. Please _____ yourself in a professional manner.

    A. condduct   B. conduct   C. cunduct

9. Ola was a _____ of dolls.

    A. collector   B. collecter   C. colector

10. The page was _____, and we could add to it.

    A. reducable   B. redusible   C. reducible

11. You may _____ your eyes now.

    A. uncouver   B. uncovar   C. uncover

12. It is not good to _____ when you have an emergency.

    A. procrastenate   B. procrastinate   C. procrastinat

13. It would be hard to _____ a balloon under water.

    A. submerge   B. submirge   C. submerje

14. One must have a lot of education to be an _____.

    A. engineer   B. enjineer   C. enginear

15. What is the _____ of meeting a tiger in your back yard?

    A. reelity   B. reality   C. realety

16. The films were _____.

    A. irreplaceible   B. irreplacable   C. irreplaceable

17. _____ your steps to find something you've lost.

    A. Retrase   B. Retrace   C. Rettrace

18. Don't stop swimming in _____.

    A. midstream   B. midstreem   C. medstream

19. Put cornstarch in gravy to _____ it.

    A. thiken   B. thicken   C. thickun

20. Our _____ for wisdom should not be on the government.

    A. depindence   B. dependance   C. dependence

Unit 30
Part 1

Circle the letter of the correct spelling of the word.

1. My house does not have a laundry _____.

   A. choot			B. chute			C. shute

2. The place looked like _____ after the tornado.

   A. chaos			B. chaoos			C. chaose

3. I want to write with a _____ lead pencil.

   A. poynted			B. pointted			C. pointed

4. Kevin paid the _____ to ride the bus.

   A. fare			B. faer			C. fair

5. The _____ front was partially glass.

   A. biulding's			B. buildings'			C. building's

6. James could be the _____ of a limousine.

   A. chaufeur			B. chaffeur			C. chauffeur

7. I love _____ cake.

   A. choclate			B. chocolate			C. chocalate

8. When will we _____ to go to the store?

   A. leave			B. leeve			C. leav

9. Doyle has lost a lot of _____.

   A. wait			B. wate			C. weight

10. My _____ house was brick.

   A. parents'   B. parent's   C. parant's

11. The governor's mansion has a pretty _____.

   A. chandalier   B. chandelier   C. chandeleir

12. We sang in the _____ class at school.

   A. chourus   B. chorus   C. choras

13. It is _____ to learn to play a saxophone.

   A. dificult   B. diffacult   C. difficult

14. Mr. Fischer was at the town's _____.

   A. fiar   B. fair   C. fare

15. The _____ playground was nice.

   A. parks'   B. park's   C. parrk's

16. _____ is a very large city.

   A. Chicago   B. Chicigo   C. Chicagoe

17. Just _____ corn seed in the ground.

   A. berry   B. burry   C. bury

18. A _____ appears to change colors.

   A. chumeleon   B. chameleon   C. chamileon

19. Some _____ porch lights were on.

   A. houses'   B. house's   C. howses'

20. _____ the tablecloth over the table.

    A. Stratch   B. Strech   C. Stretch

21. The _____ of a college basketball team gets paid quite a bit of money.

    A. coech   B. coach   C. cooch

22. The book says Pasha's parents died of _____.

    A. cholera   B. colera   C. chollera

23. Please _____ to keep from waking the baby.

    A. wishper   B. whispur   C. whisper

Unit 30
Part 2

Circle the letter of the correct spelling of the word.

1. Did you _____ Shauna's friend?

    A. meet	B. meat	C. mete

2. Our _____ mayor had a meeting for the public in November.

    A. towns'	B. town's	C. toun's

3. David was the real _____ over Goliath.

    A. champeon	B. champion	C. chammpion

4. Did you have an _____ for the boat?

    A. anker	B. angchor	C. anchor

5. One piano player seemed to play _____ than the other.

    A. noisier	B. noisyer	C. noyser

6. We can _____ for Ben to call.

    A. wait	B. weight	C. wate

7. We went to my _____ house in Tennessee.

    A. friends	B. freind's	C. friend's

8. Sue wanted to be _____ for her team.

    A. chearing	B. cheering	C. cheereng

9. Have you had a _____ to research the price of the bed?

    A. chance	B. chanse	C. chanze

10. It seems _____ to me to make a dress.

    A. semple   B. simpel   C. simple

11. The boy's _____ was bigger than the tape measure.

    A. waste   B. waist   C. waest

12. The _____ siding is blue.

    A. howse's   B. houses   C. house's

13. We should have _____ for everyone.

    A. chareity   B. charity   C. charety

14. Which _____ did Zach play in the program?

    A. character   B. charater   C. charactor

15. I did not want the dress to _____.

    A. shrenk   B. shrink   C. shringk

16. We went to the _____ department of the store.

    A. meet   B. mete   C. meat

17. The _____ cages should be kept clean.

    A. animal's   B. animals'   C. anemals'

18. Cindy did _____ the bed.

    A. perchase   B. purchese   C. purchase

19. Was Albert Einstein a _____?

    A. chemist   B. chimest   C. chemast

20. Donna used to talk _____ than Kevin did.

    A. queiter   B. quiter   C. quieter

21. The _____ of my shoe was torn.

    A. soul   B. sole   C. soel

22. The _____ singing was inspiring.

    A. group's   B. groups   C. groop's

Unit 30
Part 3

Circle the letter of the correct spelling of the word.

1. Do you want to _____ your name?

   A. chanje   B. changee   C. change

2. Working with a _____ can be dangerous.

   A. chemical   B. chimical   C. chemacal

3. When do you expect them to _____?

   A. arrive   B. arive   C. arriev

4. I wanted to use _____, solid color material.

   A. plane   B. plaine   C. plain

5. The twin _____ houses were both brick.

   A. brother's   B. brothers'   C. bruthers'

6. Which candidate did you _____?

   A. chouse   B. choose   C. choos

7. _____ Mike was a reasonable man.

   A. Chef   B. Chefe   C. Cheff

8. The end of some ink pens are _____.

   A. rownded   B. rowended   C. rounded

9. What kind of _____ do you like best?

   A. beary   B. bury   C. berry

299

10. Everyone should prepare their _____ to go to Heaven.

    A. soal   B. soul   C. sole

11. Would you like to see the judge's _____?

    A. chamber   B. chameber   C. chambur

12. Jesus _____ is the Son of God.

    A. Chriest   B. Christ   C. Christe

13. I did not want to _____ the glass plate.

    A. brake   B. braik   C. break

14. _____ the papers together with a staple.

    A. Attach   B. Attache   C. Atach

15. Did the _____ for the capital live in Frankfort?

    A. archatect   B. arkitect   C. architect

16. Some people should learn to not _____ money.

    A. waist   B. waste   C. wastte

Unit 30
Part 4

Circle the letter of the correct spelling of the word.

1. Many _____ playground equipment is made of plastic.

    A. park's B. parks' C. parks

2. The Bible teaches we should go to _____.

    A. cherch B. charch C. church

3. I felt _____ when I got the letter telling me I had been discharged.

    A. chagrin B. chagren C. chaigrin

4. A French castle is called a _____.

    A. chateao B. chateau C. chaeteau

5. _____ was a way of life for knights to live.

    A. Chevalry B. Chivalry C. Chivulry

6. The _____ of the candle was pleasant.

    A. scent B. sent C. cent

7. Many _____ exterior was damaged from the tornado.

    A. buildings B. building's C. buildings'

8. Many children look forward to _____.

    A. Christmus B. Christmas C. Christmes

9. Push on the _____ if you want the van to stop.

    A. brake B. break C. brack

301

10. Would you like to go for a ride in a _____ ?

    A. chase   B. chaze   C. chaise

11. Did you read a _____ about a liver disease?

    A. broshure   B. brochure   C. brochur

Unit 36
Part 1

Circle the letter of the correct spelling of the word.

1. He changed the _____ for his email.

    A. pasword B. password C. passwerd

2. It is not good to be a _____.

    A. scoundrel B. scowndril C. scoundral

3. I do not like for men to have a _____.

    A. beared B. beard C. bered

4. We have bought several _____.

    A. pianoes B. peanos C. pianos

5. I like to eat _____ at night.

    A. popcorn B. poppcorn C. popcron

6. Molly got into a _____ and made it safely to the Carpathia.

    A. lifboat B. lifebote C. lifeboat

7. The _____ is the shoulder blade.

    A. scapela B. scapula C. scapala

8. We should _____ to be more like Jesus.

    A. yeurn B. yearn C. yern

9. How many _____ had Mike played?

    A. banjos B. benjos C. banjoes

10. We like to eat honey wheat _____.

    A. bred					B. braed				C. bread

11. Sleeping _____ in December could be very cold.

    A. outdores				B. owtdoors				C. outdoors

12. We could make a volcano for a _____ experiment.

    A. scientifick			B. scientific			C. sientific

13. I am not _____ when I see a big dog.

    A. fearless				B. fereless				C. fearliss

14. James bought many steak _____.

    A. knives				B. knifes				C. knievs

15. A _____ is like a big deer.

    A. mous					B. moos					C moose

16. Richard hired a _____ to lay the bricks on the front of the church.

    A. brecklayer			B. bricklayer			C. briklayer

17. Biology is a branch of _____.

    A. science				B. sciense				C. sceince

18. The jurors were to stay _____ so they could be found easily.

    A. nereby				B. nearby				C. nearbye

19. Earl has repaired or replaced many _____.

    A. roofes				B. rooves				C. roofs

20. I love to eat _____ for breakfast.

    A. baecon   B. bacun   C. bacon

21. Patti and Kevin like to watch a _____ game of the University of Kentucky.

    A. basketball   B. baskitball   C. baskettball

22. Jimmy likes to ride a _____.

    A. skooter   B. scooter   C. schooter

23. I worked in _____ to finish the book.

    A. earnest   B. ernest   C. earnist

24. James grew _____ in his garden.

    A. tomatos   B. toematoes   C. tomatoes

25. I ate _____ for breakfast because it was warm.

    A. oatmeal   B. otemeat   C. oatmill

Unit 36
Part 2

Circle the letter of the correct spelling of the word.

1. Mr. Siebel owned the _____ in Fairdale.

    A. dragstore
    B. drugstor
    C. drugstore

2. I do not like to _____ the children.

    A. scold
    B. skold
    C. scolde

3. We went to the hardware store very _____ in the morning.

    A. erly
    B. early
    C. earrly

4. April is the month for many _____ to form.

    A. torenados
    B. tornadoes
    C. tornnadoes

5. _____ is made by bees.

    A. Honey
    B. Honie
    C. Honney

6. A _____ is a beautiful bird.

    A. blewjay
    B. blujay
    C. bluejay

7. Some people _____ to make others feel bad.

    A. condiscend
    B. condescend
    C. condesend

8. Was it a _____ that Eve ate?

    A. pear
    B. pare
    C. pair

9. I wanted mashed _____ for the dinner.

    A. potaetoes
    B. potatos
    C. potatoes

10. Donna likes to eat _____ leaves.

   A. spinech B. spinnach C. spinach

11. I didn't mind working _____.

   A. dountoun B. downtown C. dountown

12. Would you _____ the meeting to us?

   A. describe B. discribe C. descriebe

13. I was _____ after not getting much sleep.

   A. weary B. wairy C. wery

14. Vernon and Deb had different religious _____.

   A. believes B. beleifs C. beliefs

15. I like to eat _____ and meatballs.

   A. spagetti B. spaghetti C. spagheti

16. We went shopping again in the _____.

   A. affternoon B. afternoon C. afternoun

17. The huge cross made the _____ beautiful.

   A. scenery B. scenury C. senery

18. Most of my _____ went into a savings account.

   A. ernings B. earrnings C. earnings

19. _____ can be heard if you yell in the mountains.

   A. Eckoes B. Echos C. Echoes

20. Some men like to fish for _____.

   A. trout   B. trowt   C. troot

21. Didn't Harriet Tubman work with the _____ railroad?

   A. undergrownd   B. underground   C. undirground

22. They put a _____ robe on Jesus.

   A. scarelet   B. scarlit   C. scarlet

23. How many _____ does a transmission have?

   A. geers   B. gears   C. geares

24. Were there many _____ in one tribe?

   A chiefs   B. chieves   C. chieffs

25. Lee likes to eat _____ with cheese.

   A. brocooli   B. brocoli   C. broccoli

Unit 36
Part 3

Circle the letter of the correct spelling of the word.

1. Many children like to go outside _____.

    A. barefoot	B. bearfoot	C. bairfoot

2. Make a _____ to keep birds from eating your garden.

    A. scaircrow	B scarecrow	C. scarecroe

3. Stephanie's puppy was not a _____ yet.

    A. yereling	B. yearling	C. yeerling

4. We had two _____ in our room.

    A. radioes	B. radeoes	C. radios

5. I saw several _____ in the field.

    A. cattle	B. catle	C. cattel

6. I sewed a ruffle on the _____.

    A. bedspred	B. bedsprede	C. bedspread

7. You might _____ the shirt if you leave the iron on it too long.

    A. scorch	B skorch	C. scorech

8. The water was _____.

    A. clere	B. cleer	C. clear

9. _____ look like flutes.

    A. Picolas	B. Piccolos	C. Piccoloes

311

10. Jordan was amazed to see the _____.

   A. sheepe   B. sheep   C. sheap

11. Jonathan seemed to be a _____.

   A. chatterbox   B. chatirbox   C. chaterbox

12. I would not want to be stung by a _____.

   A. scorpeon   B. scorpiun   C. scorpion

13. I _____ the phone ring.

   A. herd   B. haerd   C. heard

14. _____ are members of the violin family.

   A. Celloes   B. Cellos   C. Celoes

15. Denise likes to hunt _____.

   A. dear   B. deer   C. dere

16. I used a _____ to hold the hat in place.

   A. hairpin   B. harepin   C. hairpen

17. Were you at the _____ at the time of the accident?

   A. seen   B. sene   C. scene

18. We went to a class to _____ more about a computer.

   A. learn   B. lern   C. laern

19. Some _____ are made by seawater.

   A. clifs   B. cliffs   C. cliffes

20. We usually eat _____ bread.

   A. wheet   B. whete   C. wheat

Unit 36
Part 4

Circle the letter of the correct spelling of the word.

1. Ben wanted to feed the _____ .

    A. goeldfish　　　　B. goldfish　　　　C. godefish

2. Try grafting a _____ from a pear tree into an apple tree.

    A. scione　　　　B. sion　　　　C. scion

3. Grandchildren should be very _____ to their grandparents.

    A. dear　　　　B. deer　　　　C. dere

4. Did you see any _____ when you visited the ocean?

    A. reefs　　　　B. reefes　　　　C. reafs

5. Some people like to eat _____ .

    A. shremp　　　　B. shrimps　　　　C. shrimp

6. If you read it daily, the Bible will lead you into the right _____ .

    A. patway　　　　B. pathway　　　　C. pathwae

7. A _____ is like a short story of something that could happen.

    A. scenareo　　　　B. scenario　　　　C. scenairio

8. Jordan was _____ a black bow tie in the wedding.

    A. wearing　　　　B. waring　　　　C. wairing

9. Many military men have been regarded as _____ .

    A. heros　　　　B. heroes　　　　C. heeroes

10. _____ is more expensive than margarine.

   A. Buter   B. Buttar   C. Butter

11. Mr. Johns had an _____ motor for his boat.

   A. outbored   B. owtboard   C. outboard

12. Many years ago a person who could read and write was called a _____.

   A. scribe   B. scrieb   C. schribe

13. I could _____ planes early in the morning.

   A. here   B. hear   C. heer

14. How many _____ did David have when he was a shepherd?

   A. stavs   B. stafs   C. staffs

15. Have you ever eaten _____?

   A. zucchini   B. zuchuni   C. zucchuni

16. James built a big _____ many years ago.

   A. birdhouse   B. berdhouse   C. birdhowse

17. It looked as if the skiers had begun their _____ of the slope.

   A. discent   B. descent   C. desent

18. Did Wendell _____ to be sick?

   A. apear   B. appeer   C. appear
19. _____ do not seem to place much value on other's belongings.

   A. Thiefs   B. Thieves   C. Thieffs

20. I have never caught a _____ in the ocean.

   A. haddock   B. hadock   C. hadduck

Unit 1

page 5
A. 1. crane 2. erase B. 1. complain 2. grain
   3. behave 4. celebrate   3. daily 4. sprain
   5. retake   5. faith

C. 1. obey 2. they

D. 1. neighbor 2. freight 3. eight 4. sleigh

E. ache F. nature

---

page 6
A. 1. neighbor 2. obey B. 1. eight 2. sprain
   3. nature 4. daily   3. grain 4. crane
   5. freight   5. sleigh 6. they
       7. ache 8. faith

C. 1. com-plain 2. e-rase 3. be-have
   4. cel-e-brate 5. re-take

D. 1. daily 2. freight 3. neighbor 4. sleigh

---

page 7
1. sprain 2. nature 3. grain 4. faith
5. sleigh 6. daily 7. freight 8. celebrate
9. crane 10. erase 11. obey 12. behave
13. complain 14. neighbor 15. retake 16. ache
17. eight 18. they

315

Unit 2

page 12
A. 1. complete   2. concrete

B. 1. displease   2. disease   3. beneath   4. grease
    5. peach   6. feast

C. 1. steeple   2. indeed

D. 1. receive   2. ceiling   3. neither

E. 1. chief   2. believe

F. 1. legal   2. fever   G. police

---

page 13
A. 1. believe   2. concrete   B. 1. peach   2. indeed
    3. chief   4. feast   3. receive   4. grease
    5. disease   6. complete   5. displease   6. ceiling

C. 1. beneath   2. fever   3. legal
    4. neither   5. police   6. steeple

---

page 14
1. steeple   2. Police   3. grease   4. ceiling
5. concrete   6. complete   7. Neither   8. fever
9. displease   10. receive   11. chief   12. legal
13. feast   14. disease   15. beneath   16. believe
17. peach   18. indeed

Unit 3

page 19

A. 1. nineteen 2. divide 3. polite 4. ninety

B. 1. lightning 2. slight

C. 1. spy 2. multiply 3. reply
4. type 5. style

D. 1. bicycle 2. pirate 3. title 4. spider
5. silence 6. triangle 7. vitamin

E. 1. i a e 2. i e y
3. i a i 4. i y e

---

page 20
A. 1. bi ' - cy - cle 2. light ' - ning 3. di – vide '
4. pi ' - rate 5. vi ' - ta - min 6. tri '- an - gle

B. 1. spider 2. nineteen 3. polite
4. title 5. ninety 6. multiply
7. silence 8. style 9. slight
10. reply 11. type 12. spy

---

page 21
1. spider 2. lightning 3. type 4. bicycle
5. multiply divide (These can be in either order.)
6. ninety 7. triangle 8. silence 9. polite
10. style 11. spy 12. reply 13. pirate
14. title 15. nineteen 16. slight 17. vitamin

Unit 4

page 26

A. 1. postpone   2. grove

B. 1. roam   2. roast

C. 1. thrown   2. growth   3. hollow
   4. arrow   5. shallow

D. 1. grocery   2. total   3. jumbo   4. focus
   5. quotation   6. locate   7. studio   8. lotion

E. 1. golden   2. postpone

F. postpone

---

page 27

A. 1. locate   2. grocery   3. arrow   4. grove
   5. shallow   6. roast   7. hollow   8. jumbo

B. 1. quotation   2. golden   3. roam
   4. total   5. focus   6. studio
   7. growth   8. lotion   9. postpone
   10. thrown

---

page 28

1. quotation   2. jumbo   3. locate   4. golden
5. thrown   6. postpone   7. shallow   8. focus
9. total   10. hollow   11. grove   12. grocery
13. roam   14. growth   15. roast   16. arrow
17. studio   18. lotion

Unit 5

page 33

A. 1. salute 2. introduce 3. tune 4. June

B. 1. stew 2. blew 3. crew

C. 1. loose 2. poodle 3. tooth 4. foolish

D. 1. truth 2. duty

E. canoe

F. group

G. 1. fruit 2. clue 3. suitcase

---

page 34

A. 1. truth 2. tune 3. poodle 4. canoe
   5. fruit 6. clue 7. June 8. stew

B. 1. du ' - ty 2. sa – lute ' 3. in - tro – duce '
   4. suit ' - case 5. fool ' - ish

C. 1. adj. 2. verb 3. noun 4. noun 5. noun 6. adj.

D. 1. canoe 2. clue 3. group 4. stew

---

page 35

A. 1. loose tooth 2. duty truth
   3. blew stew 4. foolish poodle
   5. fruit suitcase 6. tune June

B. 1. canoe 2. crew 3. introduce
   4. clue 5. salute 6. group

319

Spelling Review 6- 5th grade
(answers)

Part 1	Part 2	Part 3	Part 4
1. B	1. C	1. A	1. C
2. A	2. A	2. B	2. B
3. B	3. B	3. A	3. C
4. C	4. B	4. C	4. B
5. A	5. C	5. C	5. A
6. C	6. C	6. B	6. A
7. B	7. A	7. B	7. B
8. C	8. B	8. A	8. A
9. A	9. A	9. C	9. B
10. B	10. B	10. A	10. C
11. B	11. C	11. B	11. C
12. A	12. B	12. A	12. A
13. C	13. A	13. B	13. B
14. C	14. C	14. C	14. A
15. B	15. A	15. C	15. C
16. C	16. B	16. B	16. B
17. C	17. B	17. A	17. B
18. A	18. C	18. B	18. A
19. B	19. A	19. C	19. C
20. A	20. B	20. B	20. C
21. C	21. C		
22. A	22. B		
23. C	23. A		
24. B	24. A		
25. A	25. C		

Unit 7

page 41
A. 1. airline   2. repair   3. millionaire

B. 1. apartment   2. cargo   3. alarm   4. harness
   5. target   6. farther   7. harbor   8. pardon
   9. argue   10. spark

C. 1. careless   2. spare   3. flare   4. compare

D. aquarium

E. 1. harness   2. careless   3. millionaire

---

page 42
A. 1. flare   2. alarm   3. aquarium
   4. spark   5. target   6. harness

B. 1. repair   2. careless   3. farther

C. 1. harbor   2. pardon   3. cargo   4. spare   5. argue

D. 1. a - part - ment   2. air - line
   3. com - pare   4. mil - lion - aire

---

page 43
   1. farther   2. repair   3. target   4. apartment
   5. airline   6. millionaire   7. alarm   8. spare
   9. cargo   10. argue   11. compare   12. harbor
  13. aquarium   14. harness   15. careless   16. pardon
  17. flare   18. spark

Unit 8

page 48
A. 1. service 2. nerve 3. clerk 4. verse
5. alert 6. detergent

B. 1. surfboard 2. curly 3. curve 4. purse
5. injure 6. purple

C. 1. birth 2. flirt 3. thirteen

D. 1. search 2. research

E. journey

---

page 49
A. 1. flirt 2. nerve 3. birth 4. verse
5. curve 6. purse 7. search 8. clerk

B. 1. surf - board 2. ser - vice 3. in - jure
4. re - search 5. thir - teen 6. jour - ney
7. a - lert 8. pur - ple 9. de - ter - gent

C. 1. clerk - noun 2. purple - adj. 3. curly - adj. 4. thirteen - adj

---

page 50
1. journey 2. verse 3. thirteen 4. birth
5. curve 6. curly 7. detergent 8. purse
9. injure 10. alert 11. flirt 12. nerve
13. service 14. clerk 15. purple 16. surfboard
17. search 18. research

Unit 9

page 55
A. 1. sword 2. chores 3. bore 4. force 5. pork

B. 1. shorten 2. explore 3. seashore 4. forty
   5. orbit 6. northern 7. normal 8. forbid
   9. orchard 10. support 11. border

C. portable

D. ordinary

E. 1. word 2. short 3. fort
   4. or 5. for 6. north

---

page 56
A. 1. orbit 2. pork 3. chores 4. ordinary
   5. sword 6. bore 7. orchard 8. shorten

B. 1. forty 2. seashore 3. border 4. portable
   5. explore 6. northern 7. support 8. force

C. 1. normal 2. forbid

---

page 57
A. 1. chores 2. explore 3. normal (or) ordinary 4. border
   5. forty 6. normal (or) ordinary 7. forbid 8. force
   9. bore 10. sword 11. shorten 12. support

B. 1. portable seashore
   2. pork orchard
   3. orbit Northern

323

Unit 10

page 62

A. 1. cause 2. because 3. haul 4. automatic
   5. laundry 6. author 7. autumn 8. automobile

B. 1. awful 2. sawdust 3. paws 4. sawmill

C. 1. brought 2. cough 3. fought
   4. ought 5. sought 6. bought

D. 1. awful 2. automatic 3. author
   4. ought 5. autumn 6. automobile

---

page 63

A. 1. author 2. automatic 3. automobile 4. autumn 5. awful
   6. because 7. bought 8. brought 9. cause 10. cough

B. 1. verb 2. noun 3. noun 4. verb
   5. noun 6. noun 7. verb 8. verb

---

page 64

1. sought 2. automobile 3. paws 4. cause
5. brought 6. haul 7. sawmill 8. autumn
9. automatic 10. laundry 11. because 12. author
13. awful 14. cough 15. bought 16. sawdust
17. fought 18. ought

Unit 11

page 69

A. 1. crumble	2. stable	3. bridle	
B. 1. label	2. chisel	3. nickel	4. flannel
C. 1. capital	2. festival	3. hospital	
D. 1. major	2. alligator		
E. 1. popular	2. grammar	3. similar	
F. 1. corner	2. slipper	3. shelter	
G. 1. slipper	2. grammar	3. alligator	4. flannel

---

page 70

A. 1. la ' - bel   2. ma ' - jor   3. sta ' - ble
    4. sim ' - i - lar   5. crum ' - ble

B. 1. festival   2. hospital   3. bridle   4. shelter
    5. corner   6. slipper   7. grammar   8. alligator

C. 1. capital   2. chisel   3. flannel
    4. popular   5. nickel

---

page 71

A. 1. hospital   2. stable   3. shelter   4. similar
    5. flannel   6. major   7. festival   8. grammar
    9. popular

B. 1. chisel   2. slippers   3. capital   4. alligator
    5. nickel   6. crumble   7. bridle   8. label
    9. corner

Spelling Review 12 - 5th grade
(answers)

Part 1	Part 2	Part 3	Part 4
1. C	1. B	1. A	1. C
2. A	2. C	2. C	2. B
3. B	3. A	3. A	3. A
4. A	4. C	4. B	4. C
5. B	5. B	5. B	5. A
6. C	6. B	6. C	6. C
7. C	7. A	7. A	7. B
8. A	8. B	8. C	8. C
9. B	9. A	9. B	9. A
10. B	10. C	10. B	10. B
11. A	11. C	11. C	11. B
12. C	12. A	12. A	12. A
13. A	13. B	13. B	13. A
14. B	14. C	14. C	14. C
15. C	15. C	15. C	15. B
16. B	16. B	16. B	16. C
17. A	17. A	17. A	17. B
18. B	18. A	18. C	18. A
19. A	19. C	19. B	19. C
20. C	20. B	20. A	20. A
21. C	21. A		
22. A	22. C		
23. B	23. B		
24. A	24. A		
25. B	25. C		

Unit 13

page 77
A. 1. city 2. motorcycle 3. excellent 4. ceiling
   5. cyclone 6. circular

B. 1. geometry 2. arrange 3. judging 4. region
   5. gymnasium

C. 1. motorcycle 2. consume 3. cactus 4. customer
   5. cyclone 6. circular

D. 1. gazebo 2. guess 3. gorilla 4. August

E. 1. motorcycle 2. cyclone 3. circular

---

page 78
A. 1. arrange 2. guess 3. city 4. cactus 5. cyclone
   6. judging 7. region 8. ceiling 9. consume 10. August

B. 1. ge - om - e - try 2. go - ril - la 3. mo - tor - cy - cle
   4. ex - cel - lent 5. ga - ze - bo 6. gym - na - si - um
   7. cir - cu - lar 8. cus - tom - er

---

page 79
1. gazebo 2. gymnasium 3. region 4. judging
5. cactus 6. cyclone 7. consume 8. city
9. geometry 10. consumer 11. arrange 12. guess
13. gorilla 14. August 15. motorcycle 16. excellent
17. ceiling 18. circular

Unit 14

page 84
A. 1. lose 2. reserve 3. pleasant 4. tease
   5. visible 6. cheese 7. miserable 8. scissors
   9. busiest 10. exercise 11. chosen

B. 1. sneeze 2. zone 3. magazine

C. 1. pleasure 2. measure 3. usual 4. treasure

D. 1. visible 2. busiest 3. exercise 4. usual
   5. magazine

E. miserable

---

page 85
A. 1. miserable 2. reserve 3. treasure
   4. exercise 5. pleasant 6. scissors

B. 1. cheese - noun 2. busiest - adj. 3. lose - verb
   4. magazine - noun 5. usual - adj. 6. zone - noun

C. 1. chosen 2. measure 3. pleasure
   4. sneeze 5. tease 6. visible

---

page 86
1. chosen 2. miserable 3. busiest 4. scissors
5. tease 6. sneeze 7. lose 8. zones
9. treasure 10. pleasure 11. cheese 12. pleasant
13. exercise 14. measure 15. reserve 16. visible
17. magazines 18. usual

Unit 15

page 91
A. 1. chopper 2. benches 3. champion 4. patch
   5. channel

   B. 1. pasture 2. capture 3. natural 4. adventure

   C. 1. ancient 2. special 3. facial

   D. 1. station 2. fraction 3. patiently

E. ocean

F. 1. finish 2. shiver

G. 1. chopper 2. channel

page 92
A. 1. natural 2. chopper 3. patiently
   4. pasture 5. special 6. champion

B. 1. cap - ture 2. fa - cial 3. o - cean 4. bench - es

C. 1. adventure 2. ancient 3. capture 4. channel
   5. fraction 6. patch 7. shiver 8. station

page 93
1. chopper 2. finish 3. pasture 4. natural
5. patiently 6. patch 7. champion 8. station
9. facial 10. capture 11. ocean 12. ancient
13. special 14. benches 15. adventure 16. fraction
17. shiver 18. channel

329

Unit 16

page 98
A. 1. around 2. afar 3. distance 4. adopt
5. elementary 6. adobe 7. finally 8. certainly
9. cafeteria

B. 1. student 2. elementary 3. necessary 4. barrel
5. talent 6. cafeteria 7. refrigerator

C. 1. cousin 2. beautiful

D. 1. colony 2. ribbon

E. beautiful

---

page 99
A. 1. re - frig - e - ra - tor 2. el - e - men - ta - ry
3. caf - e - ter - i - a 4. nec - es - sar - y
5. col - o - ny 6. cer - tain - ly
7. fi - nal - ly 8. beau - ti - ful

B. 1. around 2. talent 3. cousin 4. student

C. 1. adv. 2. noun 3. verb
4. noun 5. noun 6. noun

---

page 100
A. 1. beautiful 2. Elementary 3. barrel 4. refrigerator
5. ribbon 6. student 7. adopt 8. cafeteria
9. finally 10. talent

B. 1. around 2. cousin 3. afar 4. necessary
5. colony 6. distance 7. certainly 8. adobe

Unit 17

page 105
A. 1. uniform 2. community 3. human 4. future

B. 1. jumble 2. dump 3. cuff 4. budget

C. 1. glove 2. none 3. wonder 4. shove
   5. company 6. tongue

D. 1. young 2. couple

E. excused

F. avenue

G. cummunity

---

page 106
A. 1. jumble 2. glove 3. young 4. budget
   5. none 6. cuff 7. shove 8. dump
   9. tongue 10. couple 11. human 12. wonder
   13. excused 14. future

B. 1. u - ni - form 2. com - mu - ni - ty
   3. com - pa - ny 4. av - e - nue

C. 1. community 2. company 3. couple 4. cuff

---

page 107
   1. uniform 2. community 3. future 4. dump
   5. budget 6. cuff 7. Avenue 8. wonder
   9. shove 10. excused 11. young 12. couple
   13. glove 14. tongue 15. company 16. none
   17. jumble 18. human

Spelling Review 18- 5th grade
(answers)

Part 1	Part 2	Part 3	Part 4
1. C	1. A	1. C	1. B
2. B	2. B	2. A	2. A
3. C	3. C	3. B	3. C
4. A	4. B	4. C	4. B
5. A	5. C	5. A	5. C
6. B	6. B	6. C	6. A
7. A	7. B	7. B	7. B
8. B	8. A	8. B	8. C
9. C	9. C	9. A	9. C
10. C	10. A	10. B	10. A
11. B	11. A	11. C	11. B
12. A	12. C	12. A	12. B
13. C	13. B	13. A	13. C
14. B	14. A	14. B	14. A
15. A	15. B	15. C	15. A
16. C	16. C	16. B	16. B
17. A	17. C	17. C	17. C
18. B	18. A	18. B	18. C
19. B	19. B	19. A	19. A
20. C	20. C	20. C	20. B
21. A	21. A		
22. B	22. A		
23. C	23. C		
24. B	24. B		
25. A	25. B		

Unit 19

page 113
A. 1. disapprove   2. disagree   3. discomfort   4. discourtesy
   5. dishonor

B. 1. misdirect   2. misbehave   3. misunderstand   4. misspell

C. 1. unkind   2. uncover   3. unbeatable

D. 1. irregular   2. irreplaceable

E. 1. incapable   2. inactive

F. 1. impossible   2. impure

G. irreplaceable

---

page 114
A. 1. disagree   2. disapprove   3. discomfort
   4. discourtesy   5. dishonor

B. 1. verb   2. adj.   3. verb   4. verb
   5. verb   6. adj.   7. noun   8. noun

C. 1. im - pos - si - ble   2. in - ca - pa - ble
   3. ir - re - place - a - ble   4. ir - reg - u - lar
   5. mis - un - der - stand   6. un - beat - a - ble
   7. in - ac - tive

---

page 115
A. 1. misbehave   2. disapprove   3. misunderstand   4. disagree
   5. discomfort   6. dishonor   7. unkind   8. impossible

B. 1. misdirect   2. uncover   3. irreplaceable   4. misspell
   5. unbeatable   6. discourtesy   7. irregular   8. impure
   9. incapable   10. inactive

Unit 20

page 120
A. 1. nonstop   2. nonliving   3. nonsense   4. nonresident

B. 1. enlarge   2. entangle   3. enrich

C. 1. malnourished   2. maltreat

D. 1. precook   2. prejudge   3. prepaid

E. 1. prohibit   2. procrastinate

F. 1. return   2. recall   3. retrace   4. rewrite

G. 1. nonresident   2. procrastinate

---

page 121
A. 1. entangle   2. enrich   3. malnourished
    4. maltreat   5. enlarge

B. 1. pro - cras - ti - nate   2. non - res - i - dent
    3. non - liv - ing   4. pro - hib - it

C. 1. nonsense   2. rewrite   3. retrace
    4. return   5. precook   6. nonstop
    7. recall   8. prejudge   9. prepaid

---

page 122
1. nonliving   2. precook   3. malnourished   4. nonresident
5. rewrite   6. nonsense   7. enlarge   8. prohibit
9. maltreat   10. procrastinate   11. return   12. nonstop
13. entangle   14. prejudge   15. recall   16. enrich
17. prepaid   18. retrace

Unit 21

page 127
A. 1. coauthor 2. codirectors 3. cooperate

B. 1. export 2. excuse 3. exchange

C. 1. midweek 2. midnight 3. midstream

D. 1. combine 2. compile 3. compel

E. 1. subway 2. submarine 3. submerge

F. 1. conspire 2. conceal 3. conduct

G. submarine

---

page 128
A. 1. excuse 2. combine 3. compel
   4. conceal 5. conduct

B. 1. co - di - rec - tors 2. co - op - er - ate
   3. sub - ma - rine 4. co - au - thor

C. 1. exchange 2. midstream 3. compile
   4. subway 5. conspire 6. midnight
   7. export 8. submerge 9. midweek

---

page 129
1. combine 2. midstream 3. subway 4. Excuse
5. coauthor 6. conceal 7. midnight 8. export
9. compel 10. midweek 11. exchange 12. cooperate
13. conduct 14. submerge 15. compile 16. submarine
17. conspire 18. codirectors

Unit 22

page 134
A. 1. teacher 2. baker

B. 1. actor 2. projector 3. collector

C. 1. novelist 2. scientist

D. 1. engineer 2. auctioneer

E. 1. employee 2. absentee

F. 1. golden 2. harden 3. thicken

G. 1. servant 2. assistant

H. 1. backward 2. skyward

---

page 135
A. 1. teacher 2. baker 3. actor 4. golden 5. harden
   6. thicken 7. servant 8. backward 9. skyward

B. 1. projector 2. novelist 3. collector 4. scientist 5. engineer
   6. employee 7. auctioneer 8. absentee 9. assistant

C. 1. projector 2. golden 3. harden
   4. thicken 5. backward 6. skyward

D. 1. verb 2. adv. 3. noun/ adj. 4. adj.

---

page 136
1. skyward 2. golden 3. projector 4. servant
5. novelist 6. baker 7. scientist 8. thicken
9. absentee 10. actor 11. employee 12. teacher
13. assistant 14. engineer 15. backward 16. collector
17. auctioneer 18. harden

Unit 23

page 141
A. 1. dangerous 2. courageous 3. marvelous 4. continuous

B. 1. government 2. appointment

C. 1. washable 2. dependable

D. 1. reversible 2. reducible

E. 1. importance 2. acceptance

F. 1. impressive 2. creative

G. 1. reality 2. legality

H. 1. confidence 2. dependence

---

page 142
A. 1. dangerous 2. courageous 3. marvelous
   4. confidence 5. continuous 6. creative

B. 1. reality 2. government 3. dependence
   4. importance 5. acceptance 6. appointment

C. 1. legality 2. reducible 3. reversible
   4. impressive 5. dependable 6. washable

---

page 143
1. creative 2. dangerous 3. confidence dependable
4. impressive 5. appointment 6. washable 7. reducible
8. continuous 9. courageous 10. marvelous
11. importance 12. government legality 13. acceptance
14. reality 15. dependence 16. reversible

Spelling Review 24- 5th grade
(answers)

Part 1	Part 2	Part 3	Part 4
1. C	1. B	1. A	1. A
2. A	2. A	2. B	2. C
3. B	3. B	3. C	3. B
4. B	4. C	4. C	4. B
5. C	5. A	5. A	5. C
6. A	6. C	6. A	6. C
7. B	7. C	7. B	7. A
8. A	8. B	8. B	8. B
9. C	9. A	9. C	9. A
10. C	10. A	10. A	10. C
11. A	11. C	11. C	11. C
12. C	12. B	12. B	12. B
13. B	13. B	13. A	13. A
14. A	14. A	14. C	14. A
15. B	15. C	15. C	15. B
16. C	16. A	16. B	16. C
17. B	17. B	17. A	17. B
18. A	18. B	18. C	18. A
19. B	19. C	19. B	19. B
20. C	20. A	20. A	20. C
21. C	21. B		
22. A	22. C		
23. B	23. A		

Unit 25

page 149

A. 1. cheering 2. purchase 3. check 4. champion
5. coach 6. change 7. choose 8. attach
9. charity 10. chamber 11. church

B. 1. Chicago 2. brochure 3. chauffeur 4. chandelier
5. chagrin 6. chaise 7. chute

C. 1. Chicago 2. champion 3. charity 4. chandelier

D 1. check 2. coach 3. change 4. choose
5. chaise 6. church 7. chute

---

page 150

A. 1. check 2. chaise 3. coach 4. chute
5. change 6. church 7. Chicago 8. purchase
9. attach 10. charity 11. chagrin 12. cheering
13. brochure 14. champion 15. choose 16. chauffeur
17. chandelier 18. chamber

B. 1. brochure - noun 2. check - verb
3. champion - noun 4. choose - verb

---

page 151

1. brochure 2. coach 3. church 4. chagrin
5. purchase 6. charity 7. Chicago 8. attach
9. champion 10. choose 11. chauffeur 12. chaise
13. chute 14. change 15. cheering 16. chandelier
17. check 18. chamber

339

Unit 26

page 156

A. 1. chaff   2. chance   3. chart   4. chocolate

B. 1. chateau   2. chef   3. chivalry

C. 1. chorus   2. character   3. anchor   4. chaos
   5. chameleon   6. chemical   7. chemist   8. Christ
   9. cholera   10. Christmas   11. architect

D. Christ

E. Christmas

F. chaff

---

page 157

A. 1. chaff   2. Christ   3. chaos   4. chance
   5. chart   6. chorus   7. anchor   8. chef
   9. chivalry   10. architect   11. cholera   12. chateau
   13. chocolate   14. character   15. Christmas   16. chameleon
   17. chemist   18. chemical

B. 1. chart   2. chateau   3. chef
   4. chemist   5. chocolate   6. chorus

---

page 158

A. 1. chameleon   2. Christ   3. chef   4. chance
   5. cholera   6. chateau   7. anchor   8. Christmas
   9. chorus   10. chemist   11. character   12. chart
   13. chaos   14. chaff   15. chemical   16. chocolate
   17. chivalry   18. architect

Unit 27

page 163
A. 1. sharp 2. west 3. shrink 4. shout
   5. simple 6. leave

B. 1. quieter 2. noisier
   (either way acceptable)

C. 1. inward 2. outward

D. 1. rounded 2. pointed

E. 1. noisier 2. difficult 3. quieter

F. 1. inward 2. rounded 3. arrive 4. outward
   5. whisper 6. pointed 7. simple

G. 1. east 2. leave

---

page 164
A. 1. nois - i - er 2. in - ward 3. round - ed 4. dif - fi - cult
   5. qui - et - er 6. whis - per 7. point - ed 8. sim - ple

B. 1. shout 2. shrink 3. stretch 4. whisper

C. 1. west 2. leave 3. arrive 4. east

---

page 165
1. west 2. sharp 3. arrive 4. difficult
5. stretch 6. outward 7. whisper 8. quieter
9. rounded

341

Unit 28

page 170
A. 1. sent   2. bury   3. weight   4. sole
    5. fare   6. meet   7. waist   8. plain
    9. brake

B. 1. wait   2. fair   3. plain   4. waist

C. break

D. 1. berry   2. meet

E. soul

F. 1. bury   2. berry

G. sole

---

page 171
A. 1. sole, soul   2. wait, weight   3. meet, meat
    4. waist, waste   5. sent, scent   6. bury, berry
    7. fair, fare   8. plain, plane   9. break, brake

B. 1. plane, noun   2. fair, adj.   3. meet, verb
    4. waist, noun   5. break, verb

C. 1. sole   2. soul   3. scent   4. fare

---

page 172
    1. brake   2. sole   3. Bury   4. break
    5. soul   6. scent   7. Meet   8. wait
    9. berry   10. fare   11. meat   12. plane
    13. sent   14. fair   15. waste   16. plain
    17. weight   18. waist

Unit 29

page 177
A. 1. friend's 2. house's 3. group's 4. parent's
   5. animal's 6. park's 7. brother's 8. town's
   9. building's

B. 1. friends' 2. houses' 3. groups' 4. parents'
   5. animals' 6. parks' 7. brothers' 8. towns'
   9. buildings'

C. 1. brother's 2. brothers'

D. 1. group's 2. groups'

E. 1. friend's 2. friends'

F. 1. building's 2. buildings'

page 178
A. 1. friend's 2. house's 3. town's
   4. friends' 5. houses' 6. towns'
   7. group's

B. 1. par - ents' 2. an - i - mals'
   3. broth - ers' 4. build - ings'

C. 1. animal's 2. building's 3. friend's
   4. group's 5. parent's 6. park's

page 179
1. group's 2. brothers' 3. buildings'
4. friend's 5. town's 6. houses'
7. parents' 8. park's 9. animals'

Spelling Review 30 - 5th grade
(answers)

Part 1	Part 2	Part 3	Part 4
1. B	1. A	1. C	1. B
2. A	2. B	2. A	2. C
3. C	3. B	3. A	3. A
4. A	4. C	4. C	4. B
5. C	5. A	5. B	5. B
6. C	6. A	6. B	6. A
7. B	7. C	7. A	7. C
8. A	8. B	8. C	8. B
9. C	9. A	9. C	9. A
10. A	10. C	10. B	10. C
11. B	11. B	11. A	11. B
12. B	12. C	12. B	
13. C	13. B	13. C	
14. B	14. A	14. A	
15. B	15. B	15. C	
16. A	16. C	16. B	
17. C	17. B		
18. B	18. C		
19. A	19. A		
20. C	20. C		
21. B	21. B		
22. A	22. A		
23. C			

Unit 31

page 185
A.
1. word	2. ground	3. noon	4. town
5. store	6. way	7. ball	8. foot
9. boat	10. layer	11. pin	12. spread
13. jay	14. fish	15. box	16. house

B. 1. outboard   2. outdoors

page 186
1. afternoon
2. barefoot
3. basketball
4. bedspread
5. birdhouse
6. bluejay
7. bricklayer
8. chatterbox
9. downtown
10. drugstore
11. goldfish
12. hairpin
13. lifeboat
14. outboard
15. outdoors
16. password
17. pathway
18. underground

page 187
1. password
2. drugstore
3. downtown
4. bedspread
5. basketball
6. pathway
7. birdhouse
8. goldfish
9. chatterbox
10. hairpins
11. lifeboats
12. afternoon
13. barefoot
14. outdoors
15. bluejay
16. underground
17. bricklayer
18. outboard

Unit 32

page 192
A. 1. scold 2. scorch 3. describe 4. scarlet
   5. scapula 6. scooter 7. scoundrel 8. scribe
   9. scarecrow 10. scorpion

B. 1. science 2. scene 3. scientific 4. scion
   5. scenario 6. condescend 7. scenery 8. descent

C. 1. scion 2. scorpion D. scooter

E. 1. science 2. scientific 3. describe 4. scion
   5. scribe

---

page 193
1. sci - ence 2. sci - en - tif - ic 3. scor - pi - on
4. scar - let 5. sci - on 6. sce - nar - i - o
7. scap - u - la 8. scare - crow 9. scen - er - y
10. con - de - scend

B. 1. scorch 2. scooter 3. scoundrel 4. scribe
   5. describe 6. descent 7. scene 8. scold

---

page 194
1. scoundrel 2. science 3. scarlet 4. descent
5. scorch 6. scenery 7. scorpion 8. describe
9. scenario 10. scold 11. scapula 12. scientific
13. scribe 14. condescend 15. scene 16. scarecrow
17. scion 18. scooter

Unit 33

page 199

A. 1. yearn	2. earnest	3. learn	4. earnings
5. early	6. heard		

B. 1. weary	2. dear	3. fearless	4. gears
5. beard	6. hear	7. nearby	8. appear
9. clear	10. yearling		

C. 1. pear   2. wearing

D. 1. earnings   2. wearing   3. yearling

E. 1. weary   2. early

F. nearby

---

page 200

1. yearn	2. pear	3. dear
4. learn	5. gears	6. beard
7. hear	8. clear	9. heard

B. 1. wea - ry	2. ear - nest	3. fear - less
4. earn - ings	5. wear - ing	6. ear - ly
7. near - by	8. ap -pear	9. year - ling

C. 1. earnest   2. yearn   3. earnings

---

page 201

1. weary	2. yearn	3. nearby	4. fearless
5. earnings	6. beard	7. early	8. heard
9. yearling	10. pear	11. earnest	12. clear
13. gears	14. hear	15. dear	16. wearing
17. learn	18. appear		

Unit 34

page 206

A. 1. chiefs   2. beliefs   3. reefs   4. roofs

B. 1. cliffs   2. staffs

C. 1. heroes   2. potatoes   3. tomatoes   4. echoes
    5. tornadoes

D. 1. banjos   2. cellos   3. radios   4. pianos
    5. piccolos

E. 1. thieves   2. knives

F. 1. cliffs   2. cellos   3. staffs   4. piccolos

---

page 207

1. ban - jos   2. be - liefs   3. cel - los
4. he - roes   5. ra - di - os   6. pi - an - os
7. po - ta - toes   8. to - ma - toes   9. pic - co - los
10. ech - oes   11. tor - na - does

B. 1. chiefs   2. cliffs   3. reefs   4. roofs
    5. staffs   6. thieves   7. knives

C. 1. echoes   2. heroes   3. pianos   4. piccolos
    5. potatoes   6. radios   7. tomatoes   8. tornadoes

---

page 208

A. 1. banjos   2. cellos   3. pianos   4. piccolos

B. 1. potatoes   2. tomatoes

C. 1. thieves   2. roofs   3. knives   4. heroes
    5. chiefs   6. tornadoes   7. radios   8. cliffs
    9. echoes   10. staffs   11. reefs   12. beliefs

Unit 35

page 213

A. 1. moose 2. sheep 3. deer

B. 1. broccoli 2. spaghetti 3. cattle 4. butter
   5. zucchini 6. haddock

C. 1. popcorn 2. oatmeal D. spinach

E. 1. sheep 2. wheat 3. shrimp

F. 1. a o 2. ea 3. ou 4. ea
   5. i 6. o e 7. o o i 8. a e i

page 214

A. 1. moose 2. sheep 3. deer 4. wheat
   5. trout 6. bread 7. shrimp

B. 1. honey 2. spinach 3. bacon 4. popcorn
   5. cattle 6. butter 7. oatmeal 8. haddock

C. 1. broccoli 2. spaghetti 3. zucchini

D. 1. haddock 2. zucchini 3. spinach 4. shrimp

page 215

A. 1. moose 2. honey 3. sheep 4. bacon
   5. deer 6. cattle 7. butter 8. trout
   9. shrimp 10. haddock

B. 1. spinach 2. broccoli 3. spaghetti 4. popcorn
   5. wheat 6. oatmeal 7. zucchini 8. bread

C. Answers will vary.

Spelling Review 36 - 5th grade
(answers)

Part 1	Part 2	Part 3	Part 4
1. B	1. C	1. A	1. B
2. A	2. A	2. B	2. C
3. B	3. B	3. B	3. A
4. C	4. B	4. C	4. A
5. A	5. A	5. A	5. C
6. C	6. C	6. C	6. B
7. B	7. B	7. A	7. B
8. B	8. A	8. C	8. A
9. A	9. C	9. B	9. B
10. C	10. C	10. B	10. C
11. C	11. B	11. A	11. C
12. B	12. A	12. C	12. A
13. A	13. A	13. C	13. B
14. A	14. C	14. B	14. C
15. C	15. B	15. B	15. A
16. B	16. B	16. A	16. A
17. A	17. A	17. C	17. B
18. B	18. C	18. A	18. C
19. C	19. C	19. B	19. B
20. C	20. A	20. C	20. A
21. A	21. B		
22. B	22. C		
23. A	23. B		
24. C	24. A		
25. A	25. C		

www.ingramcontent.com/pod-product-compliance
Lightning Source LLC
Chambersburg PA
CBHW080331170426
43194CB00014B/2523